The Nexus of Extremism and Trafficking:

Scourge of the World or So Much Hype?

Russell D. Howard
Colleen Traughber

Contents

Foreword

In a globalized and increasingly interconnected world, the transfer of information, expertise, and relationships are becoming more complex and more commonplace. The interconnectedness of criminal organizations that span not only countries but across regions of the globe is troubling. However, more troubling is the possibility of the linking of transnational criminal organizations with insurgent and terrorist organizations as addressed in this work by Brigadier General (retired) Russ Howard and Ms. Colleen Traughber. The radical ideologies propagating politically motivated violence now have the opportunity to leverage and participate in traditionally criminal enterprises. This melding of form and function provides criminals with new networks and violent extremists with new funding sources and potential smuggling opportunities.

General Howard and Ms. Traughber delve into the nexus between violent extremist elements and transnational criminal elements by first clarifying whether a real problem exists, and if so, what is the appropriate role for Special Operations Forces (SOF) in confronting it. The authors bring rigor to the subject matter by dissecting the issue of intention and opportunities of criminal organization and violent extremists. The question is confounded by the authors who note the wide variance in the motivations and opportunities of both different criminal organizations and extremist organizations. What the authors do make clear is that the trafficking of humans, weapons, drugs, and contraband (HWDC) is a natural way for the criminals and extremists to cooperate.

To bring the issue into focus, the authors systematically examine case studies dealing with the nexus between specific organizations and HWDC trafficking opportunities. Human trafficking in Europe and the former Soviet Union; weapons trafficking in the Far East, Asia, and South America for money; the narcotics trade by the Revolutionary Armed Forces of Columbia; Hezbollah and Kurdistan Workers' Party, as well as contraband smuggling of cigarettes, are all used to examine the extremist/criminal nexus. The connections become clear as the authors discuss each of the HWDC issues within the nexus; what is also clear is that often the nexus is a simple marriage of convenience.

General Howard and Ms. Traughber transition from the vignettes to how this nexus will impact SOF and interagency partners. Most importantly, the authors recognized a need for SOF to expand their mission set, and authorities to more appropriately address criminality in support of extremist groups. The authors identify issues for SOF including the traditional delineation between law enforcement activities and military activities. The findings, therefore, make a case that as SOF move into the future and are required to confront the nexus between extremists and criminals, a new definition and some deep thought need to be given to expanding SOF roles and authorities.

Kenneth H. Poole, Ed.D.
Director, JSOU Strategic Studies Department

About the Authors

Brigadier General (retired) Russ Howard is an Adjunct Professor of Terrorism Studies and Senior Research Fellow at the Monterey Institute of International Studies. He is also a Senior Fellow at JSOU and a Senior Adviser to Singapore's Home Team Academy. Previously, General Howard was the founding Director of The Jebsen Center for Counter-Terrorism Studies at The Fletcher School, Tufts University, the Head of the Department of Social Sciences and the founding director of the Combating Terrorism Center at West Point.

His previous Army positions include chief of staff fellow at the Center for International Affairs, Harvard University and commander of the 1st Special Forces Group (Airborne), Fort Lewis, Washington. Other recent assignments include assistant to the Special Representative to the Secretary General during United Nations Operations in Somalia II, deputy chief of staff for I Corps, and chief of staff and deputy commander for the Combined Joint Task Force, Haiti/Haitian Advisory Group. Previously, he was commander of 3rd Battalion, 1st Special Warfare Training Group (Airborne) at Fort Bragg. He also served as the administrative assistant to Admiral Stansfield Turner and as a special assistant to the commander of U.S. Southern Command.

As a newly commissioned officer, he served as an "A" team commander in the 7th Special Forces Group from 1970 to 1972. He left the active component and then served in the U.S. Army Reserve from 1972 to 1980. During this period he served as an overseas manager, American International Underwriters, Melbourne, Australia and China tour manager for Canadian Pacific Airlines. He was recalled to active duty in 1980 and served initially in Korea as an infantry company commander. Subsequent assignments included classified project officer, U.S. Army 1st Special Operations Command at Fort Bragg, and operations officer and company commander, 1st Battalion, 1st Special Forces Group in Okinawa, Japan.

General Howard has a Bachelor of Science in Industrial Management from San Jose State University and a Bachelor of Arts in Asian Studies from the University of Maryland. He also has a Master of Arts in International Management from the Monterey Institute of International Studies and a Master of Public Administration from Harvard University. He was an assistant professor of Social Sciences at the U.S. Military Academy and a senior service college fellow at The Fletcher School of Law and Diplomacy, Tufts University. His previous JSOU Press publications are *Intelligence in Denied Spaces: New Concepts for a Changing Security Environment* (2007), *Educating Special Forces Junior Leaders for a Complex Security Environment* (2009), and *Cultural and Linguistic Skills Acquisition for Special Forces: Necessity, Acceleration, and Potential Alternatives* (2011).

Ms. Colleen Traughber is a Foreign Service Officer at the U.S. Department of State with overseas assignments in Copenhagen, Denmark and Sana'a, Yemen. Prior to joining the State Department, Colleen was a Boren Fellow in Amman, Jordan and a graduate research assistant at the Jebsen Center for Counter-Terrorism Studies, where she investigated the links between terrorism and organized crime and participated in the Combating Terrorism Working Group of the Partnership for Peace Consortium. Previously, as a Fulbright Scholar at the Otto-Suhr Institute for Political Science at the Free University Berlin,  she researched European foreign policy, including the European response to terrorism. Ms. Traughber has work experience with the German Council on Foreign Relations, the German Parliament, and the Concordia Language Villages. She holds a Master of Arts in Law and Diplomacy from the Fletcher School, Tufts University, and a Bachelor of Arts from Carleton College.

Introduction

The word nexus, with origins from the Latin word for "to bind," signifies a connection, tie, or link. Since the mid-1990s, nexus has been used to describe various connections, ties, or linkages between terrorist and criminal trafficking groups, but these relationships have been a topic of increasing national and international security interest since the terrorist attacks of 11 September 2001. Separately, both terrorists and traffickers have concerned law enforcement, security personnel, and policymakers for decades. However, the notion that the different types of criminal organizations possess working relationships or have even joined forces with terrorist groups has moved some to contend that the nexus between the two types of criminal groups is a clear and present danger.[1]

There are more than a hundred recognized definitions of terrorism—some are short, some are long, some make sense, and others do not. In the United States, the Federal Bureau of Investigation (FBI), Department of Defense (DOD), and Central Intelligence Agency (CIA) each define terrorism differently, and the United Nations (UN) has been unable to define terrorism at all. There is no definition for illicit trafficking per se. However, there are separate definitions for the illicit trafficking of humans, weapons, drugs, and contraband. For the purposes of this monograph, terrorism is defined as violence or the threat of violence conducted against civilians for political or ideological purposes.[2] Also for this monograph, the definition of illicit trafficking is an amalgamation of several definitions and "is the receipt, possession, use, sale, transfer, or disposal of any persons or material without permission or authorization."[3]

The four most resilient sectors of organized international crime affecting state security are human, weapons, drug, and contraband trafficking (HWDC-trafficking). Often interconnected and sometimes mutually supporting, HWDC-trafficking is pervasive throughout the world. HWDC-trafficking is responsible for billions of dollars in profit earned by criminal organizations worldwide, and has been progressively more linked to the activities of violent extremist organizations including al-Qaeda and like-minded groups. Illicit trafficking also undermines democratic institutions and economic growth, directly impacting trade, transportation, and transactional systems.

Certainly, the line between criminal trafficking and terrorist organizations is often blurred. By definition, both HWDC-traffickers and terrorists engage in criminal activity. Also by definition, and as their name implies, terrorists use terrorist tactics to achieve their objectives. By contrast, HWDC-traffickers use extortion, bribery, and other intimidation activities to achieve their objectives; they may also employ terrorist tactics, but not exclusively. While there are similarities in their use of certain tactics, the motives of terrorists and HWDC-traffickers are different. Terrorists are generally driven by idealistic motives, however misguided; by contrast, a trafficking organization's focus is on money and profit, clear and simple.[4]

The destabilizing effects of both terrorist and trafficking organizations are indisputable. However, experts debate the importance of the so-called nexus between HWDC-trafficking and terrorist organizations, and HWDC-trafficking's effects on international security. For example, some contend that al-Qaeda must now resort to drug trafficking because effective law enforcement and interdiction campaigns have reduced its other sources of operational funding.[5] Others, such as researchers John Rollins and Liana Sun Wyler, have contended that there is no proven connection between al-Qaeda and drug trafficking at all.[6] Dr. Jeffrey M. Bale, noted terrorism expert and professor at the Monterey Institute of International Studies, believes the nexus between criminal cartels and terrorist organizations is more "much ado about nothing" than a clear and present danger.[7] According to Bale, states have often exaggerated, and sometimes fabricated, the nexus between criminal cartels and terrorist organizations in order to justify the adoption of more aggressive security or "anti-drug" policies, and that in turn has encouraged a multitude of overly alarmist analyses concerning this hypothesized criminal-terrorist nexus (e.g., in the case of "narco-terrorism"). There is no doubt, he says, that various extremist milieus and organizations—left-wing, right-wing, ethno-nationalist, and religious—have collaborated periodically with criminal organizations and actively engaged in criminal activities like arms trafficking and drug production and smuggling. There has been an even more extensive history of collaboration between criminal organizations and corrupt government officials and intelligence operatives, not to mention components of "respectable" financial institutions, which have extensive dealings with the world's "underground economy." Among the numerous well-documented examples of the "government-criminal nexus," Bates cites the collaborations between elements of French intelligence and the Corsican Mafia; between elements of the Italian political establishment and security services with the Sicilian Mafia, the Neapolitan Camorra, or the Calabrian Indrangheta; between components of the Turkish military and intelligence services and the Turkish Mafia; between both the Guomindang and the Chinese communists and various triads; between the Pakistani military and intelligence service and Pakistani and Afghan criminal networks, including opium growers; and between U.S. intelligence agencies and the Cosa Nostra (against Castro), Burmese opium growers, and other drug traffickers in their Cold War struggle against communism.[8] According to Bale, the grim reality is that almost any entity, official or unofficial, that operates covertly or clandestinely is eventually bound to encounter and interact in some way with criminal networks that also operate in the shadows. Therefore, it is hardly surprising that collaborative agreements will sometimes develop between them on either a temporary or longer-term basis.

> ... the grim reality is that almost any entity, official or unofficial, that operates covertly or clandestinely is eventually bound to encounter and interact in some way with criminal networks that also operate in the shadows.

In short, Bates believes that claims concerning the nexus between terrorists and criminals should be viewed with appropriate skepticism, especially in the absence of verifiable evidence. He emphasizes two crucial points in this context. First, members of violent extremist groups do not trust outsiders who do not share their own ideologies and agendas, especially criminals who are primarily motivated by crass materialistic motives (and who are thus potentially capable of being bought off by the highest bidder). Second, criminal organizations would be likely to endanger their own survival and impede their ability to continue profiting from illicit activities by collaborating with high-profile terrorist groups, since they would then be targeted even more aggressively by the world's security forces. One recent example should serve to illustrate the whole problem with the widespread allegations concerning the nexus between terrorists and criminals. Since 9/11, commentators and analysts have repeatedly made alarmist claims about the hypothesized or potential collaboration between Latin American drug cartels and al-Qaeda, but there is as yet little evidence in the public domain to support such claims.[9]

However, there are at least two U.S. government organizations that do not agree with Bale's assessment regarding the importance of the criminal-terrorist relationship. For example, in its 2010 Consolidated Priority Organization Targets list, the Department of Justice reported that 29 of 63 different illicit organizations demonstrated collaboration or other close relationships with terrorist groups.[10] Also, in an October 2010 meeting with representatives from 44 countries, then U.S. National Security Advisor General James L. Jones spoke of similarities between transnational organized criminal and terrorist organizations, stating:

> Much like major terrorist organizations, criminal syndicates compartmentalize their activities so that no single person knows the details of the entire operation. Apprehending even a key figure may have little to no effect. Enterprises that once focused on particular illicit activities are increasingly diversifying their operations. If we do not act together to prevent them, these trends will only continue to intensify in the years to come. And that is something that should concern all our nations. In a world full of transnational threats, transnational crime is in an ascendant phase.[11]

While some believe the nexus may be a nonexistent or mere opportunistic "marriage of convenience," others, such as General Jones, believe that it is a significant security threat—one that could involve the successful transfer of weapons of mass destruction (WMD) material to terrorists, or present opportunities for terrorists to enter the United States via human trafficking networks.[12]

This paper sorts through the "terrorist-trafficking nexus" debate by first detailing the similarities and differences between the two groups, as mentioned in this introduction. It then explains what trafficking and terrorist groups have learned from each other and what motivates them to cooperate. Next, the paper analyzes individual HWDC-trafficking organizations and their linkages to terrorism and terrorists. Case studies detailing the relationships between and among HWDC-traffickers and terrorist organizations are provided to help put the nexus debate in perspective. Finally, the "so what" of this work is explained by highlighting the challenges and opportunities associated with prosecuting traffickers and terrorists when they work in tandem.

Similarities

HWDC-trafficking groups and terrorist organizations have much in common. They are both engaged in illicit activity and use violence, fear, and corruption in pursuit of their objectives. Traffickers and terrorist groups of all stripes prosper in failing states and denied areas where governmental controls are weak, trafficking laws are not enforced, officials are corruptible, and open or porous borders make control difficult.[13] Both groups have learned to use modern technology to communicate, train, and control their subordinates.[14] For example, international drug traffickers and terrorists are among the most prolific users of encrypted messages and computers.[15] For decades, decentralized operations have been a hallmark of major criminal organizations like HWDC-traffickers. However, since 9/11 many international terrorist organizations have decided to operate similarly, forgoing familiar hierarchical and bureaucratic structures for those that are flat, more efficient, and less vulnerable to detection.[16] After suffering a major defeat, both HWDC-traffickers and transnational terrorist groups have a capacity to regenerate themselves, often reemerging in new or unrecognizable forms.[17]

In addition to strategic similarities, HWDC-traffickers and terrorist groups use the same tactics, including money laundering techniques to process illicit profits[18] and transportation of bulk cash shipments, valuables, and personnel across the same vulnerable borders.[19] Traffickers and terrorists have the same favored currency—and it is the euro, not the U.S. dollar. Because of its rarity, the 500 euro bill is referred to as the "bin Laden,"[20] which stands preferred over the U.S. $100 "Ben Franklin" due to its higher face value, which is more efficient and space-saving.[21] Furthermore, "Traffickers and terrorists both are clandestine; they both corrupt officials at the highest levels and they both rely on shadow facilitators."[22] For example, terrorists and drug traffickers hire the same document forgers, use the same routes and bribe the same border guards while executing their illicit activities.[23]

> ... terrorists and drug traffickers hire the same document forgers, use the same routes and bribe the same border guards while executing their illicit activities.

Both types of organizations are also similar in their territorial ambition and scope. Many of the most powerful traffickers—particularly drug traffickers—and terrorist organizations now have multinational operations. In the past, criminal organizations and terrorist groups were generally sub-state actors with local interests and objectives; now, however, both types of organizations operate internationally. Organized crime has diversified, says a former Drug Enforcement Agency (DEA) agent: "it has gone global and reached macro-economic proportions."[24] Indeed, according to a UN report, "the criminal world spans the planet: illicit goods are sourced from one continent, trafficked across another, and marketed in a third."[25] Al-Qaeda is also an international phenomenon, considered by some to be the world's first truly global terrorist organization.[26] For example, al-Qaeda operatives from more than 100 different countries—including the U.S.—have been arrested in 57 countries in the world.[27] Finally, HWDC-traffickers and terrorist groups, both of which are manned and led by transnational non-state actors, owe allegiance to no state and thus are beholden to no one but themselves.[28]

Another similarity between HWDC-traffickers and terrorists involves their ability to diversify their activities. In order to evade law enforcement, both groups have become increasingly innovative with their operations, expanding activities to include contraband trafficking.

Criminal and terrorist groups have also both exploited the tactic of hostage taking to generate funds. According to one major news outlet, al-Qaeda in the Islamic Maghreb "has sustained itself since 2003 primarily on revenues derived from the business of hostage taking, mostly Westerners … [the] group's kidnap-for-ransom business, especially in North Africa, generates many millions of dollars."[29] This tactic has even been discussed by the UN Security Council; in September 2010, British Foreign Secretary William Hague told the body that the British government "believes that we must act to prevent kidnap ransoms becoming a significant source of terrorist finance."[30] Indeed, organized criminal groups have been profiting from kidnapping for ransom for decades. Conservative estimates place the "market value" of this industry at well over $500 million each year[31]—a figure not lost on terrorist groups.

Differences

Despite their many similarities, criminal drug traffickers and transnational terrorists also differ in several important ways. Terrorists—at least in their own minds—are idealists: they believe they are serving a cause to achieve greater benefit for a certain constituency.[32] A criminal organization generally serves no cause other than creating wealth for itself. Terrorists seek publicity, while criminals do not; "the media collectively constitute terrorism's oxygen."[33] Terrorists often give interviews to journalists, post videos to claim responsibility for attacks, and celebrate mass media coverage of their terrorism. Conversely, organized criminals target elements of the media. In fact, Reporters Without Borders has called organized crime the media's leading predator, claiming that in the 2000s, "141 journalists have been killed for reporting on organized crime."[34] Terrorist groups are overall less likely to pursue this kind of systematic targeting of the media.

There are other differences in what terrorists and traffickers target. By definition, civilians are the terrorists' primary target, while for drug traffickers, they are customers. Terrorist victimization tends to be less discriminate than the violence used by organized criminals.[35] That is not to say that the perpetrators of organized crime would weep at the victimization of an innocent bystander; however, they are slightly more concerned than a terrorist might be with such an outcome. By contrast, traffickers—particularly drug traffickers—target other traffickers as a way of eliminating competition; they also target police and military to instill fear against arrest and prosecution. Finally, criminal traffickers such as the drug cartels in Mexico fight each other in turf wars, which is less common with rival terrorist groups.[36]

Scholar Bruce Hoffman sums it up best: most fundamentally, he says, the criminal is not concerned with influencing or affecting public opinion: he simply wants to abscond with money the easiest way possible. "By contrast," he says, "the aim of terrorists' violence is ultimately to change 'the system'— about which the ordinary criminal could care less."[37]

Learning from Each Other

While the differences are fundamental and are not meant to be dismissed as "minor," the similarities between terrorist and organized criminal groups highlighted in paragraphs above showcase these entities' ability to adapt, strengthen, and often learn from each other's successes and failures. As illustrated by one quintessential example, this phenomenon is not new:

> The traditional Mafia has learned to use the magnifying glass of
> symbolic violence to reach a wider audience: in 1993, the Sicilian
> Mafia carried out a series of car bomb attacks in the Italian mainland
> … plans were laid to blow up the Leaning Tower of Pisa. The aim

was not to eliminate an enemy, but to intimidate public opinion and Parliament into abrogating recently passed anti-mafia legislation.[38]

In this instance, the Italian Mafia clearly adopted "terrorist" tactics to achieve an objective. Criminal groups in Brazil have also realized the potential effectiveness of using terror tactics to force political demands on the government, especially when the state threatens their illicit operations.[39] For example, following the inauguration of a new Brazilian government administration in 2002, the increasing power of Brazilian drug traffickers prompted the new administration to clamp down on them—particularly those operating out of Rio de Janeiro. The tougher restrictions provoked these criminal groups into "launching a campaign of political violence."[40] This strategy resulted in group members who "bombed buses, fired shots at government buildings, and targeted police officers," with the violence ending "only after the state appeared to grant the criminal group leaders immunity in order to continue conducting their criminal operations with limited obstacles."[41] Two ominous tactics recently adopted by Mexican drug cartels point to the cross-fertilization of ideas and perhaps training from terrorist organizations such as al-Qaeda. A relatively new tactic used by drug traffickers in Mexico, and evidenced now in the United States, is beheading.[42] At least 40 people were decapitated in Mexico in 2008, two years after the method emerged in the country. According to Jorge Chabat, a criminal justice expert at the Center for Research and Teaching of Economics in Mexico City, drug trafficking bosses "saw internet video of beheadings of hostages captured by Muslim extremists in Iraq and Pakistan, and adopted the tactic themselves, down to the posting of video on the internet" and violent display of the victims' dismembered heads.[43] Beheadings also now appear to have reached U.S. territory; the first known beheading conducted by drug criminals in the United States occurred in Phoenix, Arizona in March 2011.[44]

Another terrorist tactic copied by traffickers is the use of improvised explosive devices (IEDs), particularly car bombs. Presently, Mexican drug traffickers fighting security forces use the same kind of IEDs that insurgents and terrorists employ against coalition forces in Afghanistan and Iraq.[45] During the last three months of 2010, Mexico witnessed "at least three vehicle-borne explosive devices against [its] security forces, which look very similar to the model that we saw in Iraq and continue to see," said Lieutenant General Michael Oates, former director of the Joint IED Defeat Organization.[46]

In July 2010, an IED car bomb attack in Juarez, Mexico was the first example of a suicide attack used by a trafficking organization. Responding to what they thought was an "officer down" emergency call, a nearby police-man and paramedic worked frantically to save what they thought was another policeman's life. Unfortunately, the "wounded officer down" was a decoy who himself was killed with the responding police officer and paramedic when a nearby car bomb exploded.[47]

Terrorists also learn from criminal cartels. Many analysts believe that transnational terrorist organizations, including al-Qaeda, adopted their decentralized cell-and-network-based structure from drug cartels.[48] Ter-rorists have also copied techniques used by criminal organizations to hide, transfer, and launder their money and other assets. Common methods for both criminal and terrorist groups include the use of alternative remittance systems, such as the hawala system in the Middle East and South Asia and the Asia/Oriental system used by Chinese Triads in Asia and around the world.[49] Trade-based money laundering, bulk cash smuggling, and the smug-gling of high-value goods, including precious metals and stones, are also examples of "value transfer" methodology learned by terrorists from traffick-ers.[50] More recently, there is evidence that al-Qaeda has copied "drug mule" techniques used by traffickers who cross fron-tiers with up to several pounds of illicit drugs packed in their body cavities. However, instead of ingesting drugs, al-Qaeda's technique is to ingest explosives. Weapons experts explain the "ingested explosive" technique could be effec-tive for assassinations or possibly as a weapon on a commercial airliner.[51] A video taken by al-Qaeda documents the "ingested explosive" attack conducted by 23-year-old Abdullah Hassan al-Asiri on a Saudi anti-terrorism official, which resulted in only slight injuries to the target and the death of the detonator.[52]

The examples provided illustrate knowledge transfers between trafficking groups and terrorists, and how each entity can benefit from sharing tactics.

The examples provided illustrate knowledge transfers between trafficking groups and terrorists, and how each entity can benefit from sharing tactics. While there is no hard evidence of formal exchange programs between these trafficking groups and terrorist organizations, there are clear indications that the two are observing each other and adopting techniques that might benefit their groups and further the achievement of their organizational goals.

1. The Big Four of Trafficking: Human, Weapons, Drugs, and Contraband

Human Trafficking

Human trafficking is often described as the process of recruitment and transportation of people by means of deception or force for the purpose of exploitation.[53] The exploitation can include forced labor, prostitution, or other involuntary activities. Because prostitution or domestic servitude are the most common uses for trafficked persons, the victims of human trafficking are often assumed to be mainly women and children. In reality, the victims can be men, women, children, or anyone who is transported against his or her will. Human trafficking is thus differentiated from human smuggling, in which illegal immigrants cross borders as a matter of choice.

Of the four major types of trafficking, human trafficking statistics are the least defined with any accuracy. For example, estimated profits from human trafficking range from a low of $9.5 billion a year to $42.5 billion a year.[54] The numbers of people trafficked are similarly startling—two to four million people are trafficked against their will every year, including those forcefully moved across borders and within borders.[55]

Current evidence suggests that human trafficking continues to benefit from an increasingly globalized world. Even with heightened awareness of the problem among both academics and policymakers,[56] the number of human trafficking cases increases annually as the ability of traffickers and trafficked victims to move around the globe also grows,[57] and policymakers have been unable to stem the tide of the crime. As human trafficking levels increase, so do opportunities for collusion with other forms of organized crime and violent groups. Human traffickers have been known to adopt the tactics and strategies of drug traffickers, learning from the lucrative business of the narcotics trade.[58] These tactics include moving goods (i.e. the trafficking victims) in a low-cost and high-volume manner, forming a trafficking ring with high consumption and small savings, depleting natural resources, enabling violent entrepreneurship, using trade and development strategies, and employing the methods of traditional slavery. They have shown great ingenuity in adapting their business tactics to the trafficking operating environment.[59]

Human Trafficking and Terrorism

Just as the profits from human trafficking are less than those from arms and drug trafficking, the links between this form of organized crime and terrorism are less pronounced. Nevertheless, evidence suggests that the nexus between human trafficking and terrorism is growing and, where it has taken hold, is also thriving, particularly in ungoverned spaces.[60] Specifically, human traffickers and terrorists appear to benefit from using the same routes and similar illicit financing sources.[61] In areas where both terrorism and human trafficking have thrived, the likelihood of a symbiotic relationship between human trafficking and terrorism greatly increases.

Select cases show that supporters and facilitators have actually used human trafficking to support terrorist efforts. Three Pakistani citizens—who were tried in a U.S. court—pleaded guilty to provide material support to the Tehrik-e-Taliban in Pakistan (TTP), a designated foreign terrorist organization (FTO) often referred to as the "Pakistani Taliban."[62] The three men

> ... admitted that between January 3, 2011 and March 10, 2011 they conspired to provide material support to the TTP in the form of false documentation and identification, knowing that the TTP engages in terrorist activity and terrorism. According to court documents ... [they] conducted a human smuggling operation in Quito, Ecuador that attempted to smuggle an individual they believed to be a member of the TTP from Pakistan into the United States.[63]

According to Assistant Attorney General for National Security Lisa Monaco, the case "underscores the threat posed by human smuggling networks that facilitate terrorist travel."[64]

A similar case was reported in Europe in late 2011, when a Helsinki man supporting the Somali Islamist al-Shabaab movement was arrested by Finland's National Bureau of Investigation for participating in aggravated human trafficking with a terrorist intent. The lead investigator stated that "plans were under preparation for taking people abroad without their knowledge of the real purpose of their travel. There is reason to believe that they would have been taken to a training camp."[65] This case is reportedly the country's first-ever terrorism case, showing the expansion and pervasiveness of the nexus.

In 2011, the European Police Office (Europol) reported a growing connection between human trafficking and terrorism. Its European Union (EU) Terrorism Situation and Trend Report summarized member states' intelligence and analysis that the Kurdistan Workers' Party (PKK) and the Liberation Tigers of Tamil Elam (LTTE) were actively involved in human trafficking. The Canadian government further reported that LTTE entered the human cargo business when its arms smuggling profits dried up after the war in Sri Lanka ended.[66] In August 2011, the Criminal Investigation Department of Sri Lanka arrested a leading member of the LTTE named "Uganda Bala." The human trafficker had been transiting between Malaysia, Singapore, India, Thailand, and several other countries, earning millions of rupees for LTTE by sending people to European countries via illegal means.[67] These reports not only highlight the linkages between human trafficking and terrorism, but they also show the resiliency and adaptability of these criminal nexus organizations.

Human traffickers and terrorists benefit from disruptions in an increasingly globalized world characterized by enclaves that provide space for illicit activities.[68] These spaces can be juridical, social, virtual, or territorial, and may be the result of the vacuum in power left by weak or failing states.[69] Like other forms of organized crime, human trafficking is pervasive, and there is hardly a location in the world that is not affected, whether as an origin, transit, or recipient country.[70] As a result, the opportunity for linkages and alliances between human trafficking and terrorist groups is great and widespread. The following case studies provide a sampling of this growing phenomenon.

Human Trafficking Case Study: Europe

Human trafficking in Europe ranges from human smuggling to terrorists who profit from human trafficking. In the first case, voluntary migrants, such as those in the Mediterranean and North Africa, benefit from being trafficked or smuggled to the EU southern borders. As a result of European integration and globalization in recent years, the removal of national borders has been accompanied by an increase in migration, both legally and illegally, to the EU.[71] Separated from North Africa by the Mediterranean, the southern EU countries are a natural destination point for illegal immigrants from North Africa. Due in part to its economic prosperity, the EU, in fact, is a leading net recipient of trafficking victims worldwide.[72] Increasingly, those migrants are associated with organized crime and, in some cases, terrorism.[73]

With porous borders and a relatively secure environment, Europe serves as a natural nexus for human trafficking and terrorism—a fact that is only slowly being recognized. The threat from Islamic extremists, however, is real. Foreign fighters from Morocco, for example, played an essential role in the Madrid bombings of 11 March 2004. Illegal migrants from North Africa acting as terrorists are not the only source of the threat, as another example shows; police apprehended a network of 13 would-be terrorists from Pakistan, India, and Nigeria in Barcelona on 3 February 2009.[74] The group not only forged passports, but also trafficked in human beings across Europe, including in Belgium, Britain, France, Germany, Switzerland, and even Thailand.[75]

In the second case, traffickers actually profit from human trafficking. For example, the PKK in Turkey has used human trafficking as a means of both recruitment and funding.[76] Amongst other means, the PKK has financed its operations through human trafficking.[77] The PKK also uses human trafficking networks to move clandestinely within Europe.[78] Finally, the terrorist organization has recruited members from the ranks of those trafficked.[79] Whether smuggling or trafficking, illegal migration has increasingly become a concern in Europe, due to its links to international terrorism.[80] EU security forces are shifting their focus from external threats to internal or "transnational" threats from non-state groups, including organized crime syndicates and terrorist organizations, partially as a result of human trafficking.[81] As the Europe case study suggests, however, transnational threats like human trafficking and terrorism should not be addressed unilaterally; they should be addressed in collaboration with other states and with international and nongovernmental organizations.[82]

Human Trafficking Case Study: Former Soviet Union

Russia and other parts of the former Soviet Union are well known as major transit hubs for victims of human trafficking from across the globe, including Asia, Africa, Afghanistan, Iraq, Kurdistan, and Somalia.[83] Human trafficking activities in the region are not only well established, they are growing. Yet, just as the extent of the involvement of the former Soviet Union's organized crime organizations (such as the Russian Mafia) in human trafficking is unclear,[84] the connections between human trafficking and armed extremist groups are also less distinct. There is, however, growing evidence that the two share nodes of operation, relying on the same or similar local contacts for clandestine movements and operations, whether it be for the sex trade—the most blatant form of human trafficking in post-Soviet spaces—or armed movement.[85]

In areas of the former Soviet Union, terrorists and criminals are taking advantage of the same "gray areas" in which to create an operational space. For example, in Central Asia and the Caucasus, human trafficking is growing.[86] According to the International Organization for Migration, thousands of women have been trafficked from Central Asia during the past two decades;[87] Meanwhile in the Caucasus, the estimates are even higher; each year, thousands are trafficked from and through the region.[88] At the same time, armed factions such as Chechen extremists and others in the Caucasus, Central Asia, and Russia have made use of the ungoverned areas for their own designs.[89] Where ungoverned spaces exist in these areas, both traffickers and terrorists benefit from similar nodes of operation, even if collusion is not direct.

As suggested, the connection between human trafficking and terrorism is less entrenched in Russia. While there are examples of groups, such as the Russian Mafia, engaged with both violent extremist activities and crime, including human trafficking, the relationships tend to be linkages of convenience rather than direct collusion. At the very least, human traffickers and terrorists in the Russian context tend to follow the same routes, taking advantage of the same gaps and "gray areas" of the world. For example, traffickers in both Central Asia and the Caucasus travel the same routes that are used by terrorists.[90] Employing human trafficking as a profitable, criminal enterprise appears to be one of a number of options, and is often displaced by its more lucrative alternatives, arms or drug trafficking.

Weapons Trafficking

The trafficking of weapons is commonly defined as the illegal trade of conventional arms as well as the materials necessary to construct biological, chemical, and radiological weapons. Sometimes described as "gun-running," weapons trafficking often involves small arms and light weapons. Weapons trafficking tends to have a natural affinity with armed conflict; the illegitimate purchasers are often affiliates of armed groups with nefarious intentions. As a result, the links between weapons trafficking and terrorism are entrenched.

In comparison to human trafficking, the profits from the illicit trade in weapons are more fixed, with estimates of $10 billion per year.[91] Arms trafficking, however, creates more of a "bang for the buck" than human trafficking by having the capacity to fuel transnational conflict, including terrorism. According to the Small Arms Survey, the illicit trade in small arms and light weapons involves 875 million arms around the world.[92] Small arms are often sold for money or valuable goods like diamonds, drugs, or other smuggled goods. In addition to being a profitable criminal activity, arms trafficking also has the capacity to fuel conflict, providing tangible support to hundreds of wars and insurgencies over the past two decades.

Worldwide attention to weapons trafficking, particularly concerning WMD, has risen in recent years. Despite the increased resources allocated to the problem, evidence suggests that arms trafficking levels are only rising, particularly in the small arms and light weapons market.[93] In addition, the natural affinity between arms trafficking and terrorism is often overlooked. The U.S. Government Accountability Office review of the State Department's annual *Country Reports on Terrorism* showed that, while the U.S. government is aware of terrorism safe havens around the world, it is not reporting on the actions of host governments to combat the trafficking of WMD though those safe havens, effectively ignoring the links between WMD trafficking and terrorism in areas of critical interest to national security.[94]

Weapons Trafficking and Terrorism

In contrast to human trafficking, weapons trafficking is clearly linked to terrorism, with reports of collaboration between human traffickers and terrorists on every continent.[95] The reports are both clear and far-reaching; there are not only links from insurgent groups to small arms and light weapons, but also to biological, chemical, and nuclear weapons.[96] While the links between weapons traffickers and terrorists are not as profit-motivated as other trafficking methods, the natural affinity between the two activities indicates that where one exists, the other is likely to be found.

Arms traffickers and terrorists benefit from many of the same "gaps" created by an increasingly globalized world, as do other trafficking groups. A decline in state sponsorship for terrorists at the end of the Cold War is generally considered to be a driver behind terrorist organizations' development of "in-house" criminal activities such as arms trafficking to fund operations.[97] As a result, alliances tend to be one of several types: mutual benefit between traffickers and terrorists; direct involvement of terrorists in trafficking; or replacement of the terrorists' ideological goals with the traffickers' profit motivations.[98] The relationships therefore tend to vary widely in both the extent of the collusion and the nature of the collaboration.

Arms Trafficking Case Study: Thailand

Arms trafficking, which has a natural affinity to terrorism, can be quite lucrative if the arms trafficker has the links to the right extremist organizations. Unlike human trafficking, arms trafficking is more than just a means to generate income for criminal organizations; it is also a direct source of armaments in conflict. In a globalized economy, arms recipients do not need to be in the vicinity of the arms trafficker, who can find a location that is conducive for illicit activity. Arms can be trafficked over long distances to reach their ultimate destination, given the right price.

In a Thailand-based case, notorious weapons trafficker Viktor Bout was able to sell arms to almost any organization that could pay him. He reportedly sold weapons to the Revolutionary Armed Forces of Columbia (FARC) and the Taliban, as well as warring factions in Angola, the Democratic Republic of Congo, Liberia, Rwanda, Sierra Leone, and Sudan.[99] Arrested by Thai authorities on 6 March 2008, this "merchant of death" had built a private air fleet to transport weapons from ex-Soviet stocks to the major conflicts of the world.[100]

In this case, the terror and criminal elements developed into a nexus, relying on one another for support and depending on the other for expertise.

While not directly related to an armed conflict, the case of weapons trafficker Viktor Bout shows the symbiotic relationship that can emerge between crime and terror. In this case, the terror and criminal elements developed into a nexus,[101] relying on one another for support and depending on the other for expertise. The relationship moved past the point at which the two types of groups adopted similar methods without working together, but did not progress to the sharing of methods or motives.

Arms Trafficking Case Study: Osama bin Laden

In other cases, the link between arms trafficking and terrorism is better documented. A terrorist organization may be directly involved in trafficking activities, possibly acting as a bridge between terrorism and organized crime or linking organizations that engage in each type of activity. Osama bin Laden's attempt to purchase nuclear-grade weapons material through other terrorist organizations illustrates a case of direct links between arms trafficking and terrorism. Although ultimately thwarted, the case demonstrates the extent of collusion that can develop between organizations with drastically different directives.

Bin Laden's first attempt to acquire uranium was in Sudan in 1993, prior to the bombings of the embassies in Kenya and Tanzania.[102] Reportedly unable to acquire the weapons-grade uranium in Sudan,[103] bin Laden tried again in 2000 to make a purchase, this time of "ready-made" Russian nuclear weapons from Chechen weapons traffickers.[104] Bin Laden was duped to the tune of $2 million in Sudan and possibly as much as $30 million in Chechnya for his attempt to purchase weapons-grade plutonium and/or nuclear weapons.[105]

Bin Laden's foiled plot to attain nuclear materials further demonstrates the links between crime and terror groups. In colluding with extremists in Sudan and Chechnya, bin Laden and his organization demonstrated their willingness to work with criminal syndicates for their own purposes—as well as the shrewdness of criminal groups to take advantage of a demand without delivering. Collusion like this suggests elements of a mutually beneficial symbiotic relationship with or dependence on groups that are themselves hybrid terror-crime organizations, expressing methods and motives of both.[106] Although in this case unsuccessful, such terrorist organizations have the capacity to be just as much terrorist as criminal, and should be recognized and approached by counterterrorism and law enforcement officials as such.

Arms Trafficking Case Study: Moldova

A recent example of potential coordinated cooperation between criminal syndicates and terrorists was uncovered during a June 2011 sting operation by Moldovan authorities in which police were able to pre-empt North African buyers from purchasing uranium oxide. Moldovan authorities arrested the suspects, traced the uranium to Russian facilities, and discovered data indicating the group had been actively seeking contacts in North Africa. Little is known about the North African buyer(s), but Senator Richard Lugar of the Senate Foreign Relations Committee has reported his concerns regarding the smuggling operations and their links to a region where confirmed terrorist activity is on the rise.[107] The uranium was moved through Transnistria, a breakaway republic located between the Dniester River and the eastern Moldovan border to Ukraine. It has been an ideal operating ground for smugglers, as flights into the area cannot be monitored, borders are porous, and security is weak.[108] The case not only underscores the prevalence of nuclear or radiological materials originating in former Soviet states, but also highlights the link with North Africa. This particular interdiction highlights the need to strengthen monitoring of bomb-making materials and stockpiles. Heightened security would aid in deterring future relationships between European smugglers and buyers from a region that hosts known terror cells. However, it also provides an example of successful international collaboration: Moldovan law enforcement, trained by U.S. specialists, undoubtedly enhanced the sting operation.

Arms Trafficking Case Study: Tamil Tigers

In several cases, the LTTE, or "Tamil Tigers," have been involved in arms trafficking, illustrating a clear case of a designated terrorist organization forging close relationships with criminal groups. In 2010, Balraj Naidu was convicted of providing material support to a terrorist organization. The Singapore arms broker was said to have equipped a terrorist organization with advanced weapons. U.S. Immigration and Customs Enforcement's (ICE) Homeland Security Investigations successfully investigated the case to prove that Naidu attempted to purchase weapons from China, Thailand, North Korea, the Philippines, and Indonesia for the LTTE to use against Sri Lankan government forces.[109] According to the report, Naidu's weapons source introduced him to a Maryland based undercover agent with whom he negotiated the acquisition of American-made weaponry, which were to be delivered to the Sea Tigers, the naval branch of the Tamil Tigers. Members of the terrorist organization purchased 28 tons of weapons for $900,000. Upon payment and inspection of the weapons, co-conspirators Bin Osman, Haji Subandi, Erick Wotulo, and Thirunavukarasu Varatharasa were arrested.

These arrests led to the indictment of Naidu, who was sentenced to four years and nine months in prison.[110] The acquisition of advanced weapons for the Tamil Tigers—a designated foreign terrorist organization—was found to be illegal. The case highlighted the relationship between the arms merchants and terrorist-supporting group and showed the importance of continued enforcement and vigilance of export laws.

In 2009, three members of a transnational gang were charged with brokering human trafficking, forging and selling fake passports, and transporting illegal migrants to Thailand. The arrest of Mohammad Ali Hussein, Mohammad Mudbahem, and Chubri Awae revealed that the gang was not only involved in human trafficking, earning around 200,000 baht (approximately $6,500) for each individual, but also had close ties with the LTTE in Sri Lanka and insurgents in the far south of Thailand, where terrorists were reportedly trained by Jemaah Islamiyah and al-Qaeda. The operation—carried out collaboratively between the Department of Special Investigation, armed forces, and immigration police—found that the three suspects helped terrorists and the southern insurgency movement, funding activities through their involvement with war weapons and the drug trade. According to intelligence units, the group had supplied fake passports to people who possibly included al-Qaeda members traveling to the U.S. to carry out the 9/11 terrorist attacks. Hussein is alleged to be involved in the trafficking of weapons.[111] The successful arrest therefore prevented sophisticated weaponry from getting into the hands of terrorists.

Drug Trafficking

Drug trafficking is an illegal system—a global black market consisting of the cultivation, manufacture, distribution, and sale of illegal drugs. It is a commercial exchange of illegal drugs for profit. Varying estimates of the annual income from worldwide drug trafficking range between $400 billion and $1 trillion a year.[112]

Some analysis suggests that terrorist groups such as al-Qaeda increasingly rely on drug trafficking proceeds for operational funding.[113] In any case, the sheer dollar volume generated by the illicit drug market makes rich and poor countries alike vulnerable to the money's corruptible influences. Michael Shifter, vice-president for policy at Inter-American Dialogue, a Washington, DC-based research center, said drug trafficking is "devastating" and a "major threat" to democratic governance and peace for nations around the world.[114]

Drug Trafficking and Terrorism

Experts disagree about the so-called nexus between drug traffickers and terrorist organizations. Michael Braun, former assistant administrator and chief of operations at the DEA, believes the nexus is a serious, long-term threat which increases the complexity and challenges of taking on both drug traffickers and terrorists.[115] According to Braun, the nexus between traffickers and terrorists is not a new trend, but now is growing at "light speed."[116] Braun cites DEA statistics suggesting that 19 of the 43 officially designated foreign terrorist organizations (FTOs) have links to some aspect of the global drug trade. He also believes that approximately 60 percent of terror organizations are in some way connected with the illicit narcotics trade.[117]

Others disagree and instead characterize drug trafficker-terrorist relationships as marriages of convenience that serve primarily logistical and financial purposes. According to those who support the "marriages of convenience" argument, the two groups only operate together in those relatively rare instances where there is also some ideological or political relationship.[118]

Certainly, there is disagreement with regards to al-Qaeda's participation in the drug trade. Some contend that, due to the global crackdown on al-Qaeda's funding sources, the terrorist group has increasingly turned to drugs to finance its operations.[119] Congressional Research Service researchers John Rollins and Liana Sun Wyler disagree; instead, they contend that there is no proven connection between al-Qaeda and drug trafficking at all.[120]

So who is correct? While the answer probably lies somewhere within the spectrum of differing opinions, there is recent evidence indicating Braun's scenario may be more likely—that there is a serious trend toward increased cooperation between drug traffickers and certain terrorist groups. Why? In the simplest terms: money. Terrorist organizations have chosen to participate in the illicit drug trade for several financial reasons. First, according to Michael Braun, "state sponsorship of terrorism is declining, and the Department of Treasury, CIA, ICE, and FBI have done a very good job at identifying private donors and disrupting the flows of terror financing."[121] As a result, terrorist groups "are increasingly in need of new sources of funds and the drug business fills this need perfectly."[122] Drugs provide many different revenue streams, including funds derived from taxing farmers and local cartels, and the provision of security for all aspects of production, trade, and distribution.[123] What do drug cartels get out of the relationship? One benefit is protection; another is shared intelligence, including knowledge of safe routes of passage and bribable border guards; and a third is access to an expanded market.

Drug Trafficking Case Study: the FARC

The FARC is an organization operating as both a terrorist and drug trafficking organization and has the dubious distinction of being the first to be identified as a "narco-terrorist" group. Established in the early 1960s as a Marxist group with a leftist agenda, the FARC has both pursued a political agenda within Colombia and created a viable regional and international drug trafficking network based from its Colombian stronghold.[124] In fact, the FARC has increased its influence almost entirely through the drug trade. In the 1970s, the FARC taxed marijuana growers in the rural areas it controlled. In the 1980s, the FARC moved into the cocaine business by taxing coca plantations in areas under its control. By 2010, the FARC had replaced the defeated Cali and Medellin drug cartels to the extent that General Cesar Pinson, head of the Colombian police force's anti-narcotics section, now calls the FARC "the big cartel."[125] The FARC nets an estimated $300 million a year[126] from the drug trade and is actively working with Mexican traffickers who import drugs from Colombia.[127]

In November 2011, Alfonso Cano, head of the FARC, was killed by the Colombian army, marking a major turning point for the organization. However, questions remain pertaining to what the death of the leader will mean for the terrorist group and the war against it.[128] The FARC has suffered losses of leadership in the past—most notably the killing of founder Manuel Marulanda in 2008 and the death of top commanders Raul Reyes in 2008 and Jorge "el Mono Joy Joy" Briceno in 2010—but has survived as others have stepped up to take control.[129] For the present, all available evidence suggests that the FARC continues to use its drug profits to support terrorist operations in Colombia.[130]

Drug Trafficking Case Study: Hezbollah

Hezbollah directly benefits from drug trafficking. Indeed, Hezbollah is not new to the drug trafficking business, having moved opiates out of Lebanon's Bekaa Valley for decades.[131] Despite the fact that poppy cultivation has declined in the Bekaa Valley,[132] the organization still benefits from selling illicit drugs in the Middle East, particularly to Israeli Arabs, in exchange for money or information. For example, in 2002, a lieutenant colonel in the Israeli Army was charged with spying for Hezbollah in exchange for hashish and heroin.[133]

Hezbollah is currently increasing its involvement in the drug trade because of a shortfall in operational funds. The estimated $120-200 million annual stipend from Iran has not met Hezbollah's operational requirements. Moreover, there is some evidence that Hezbollah will need to generate even more revenue from drug trafficking, as Iran is hard-pressed to maintain funding at past levels.[134] Indeed, much of Hezbollah's additional support comes from drug trafficking, a major moneymaker surprisingly endorsed by Iranian Mullahs through a particular fatwa.[135] In addition to long-standing Bekaa Valley drug trafficking, Hezbollah is now trafficking cocaine from Latin America for the FARC from Colombia, through Venezuela, and on to West Africa, where it is shipped to Europe and the Middle East.

> According to reports from Interpol and the United Nations, cocaine transported from Venezuela and traded through West Africa accounts for a considerable portion of terrorist group Hezbollah's income. Hezbollah takes advantage of the Lebanese Shiite expatriate Diasporas in South America and West Africa to guarantee an efficient connection between the two continents.[136]

According to Rudy Atallah, a former Africa counterterrorism director for the U.S. DOD, Hezbollah's tentacles have spread across West Africa. Starting from Senegal, says Atallah,[137] "they have a vast array of connections with the drug dealers, so it's a natural flow where you have facilitations by Hezbollah in Africa to move drugs coming from Latin America to West Africa and up into Europe."[138] Once the drugs hit Europe, Hezbollah continues its trafficking operations. For example, German police arrested two Lebanese citizens living in Germany in October 2009 after they transferred large sums of money to a family in Lebanon with connections to Hezbollah's leadership, including known Hezbollah terrorist and the group's Secretary General, Hassan Nasrallah. Officials suspected that the duo was selling cocaine in Europe and sending the profits to Lebanon, ostensibly to support Hezbollah.[139]

Unfortunately, proving Hezbollah complicity in drug trafficking is often difficult. On 28 April 2009, 17 people were arrested in Curaçao for alleged involvement in a drug trafficking ring that had connections to Hezbollah. The suspects included four from Lebanon and others from Curaçao, Cuba, Venezuela, and Colombia. According to police reports at the time, some of the drug trafficking proceeds were funneled through informal Middle Eastern banks to Hezbollah.[140] According to Curaçao prosecutor Ludmila Vicento, "We have been able to establish that this group has relations with international criminal organizations that have connections with the Hezbollah."[141] Additional details later emerged:

> The suspects are reported to have specialized in exporting Colombian cocaine that they obtained from smugglers who transported the drugs to Curaçao using speedboats and ocean-going cargo ships that embarked from Venezuela. The drug ring is also reported to have imported arms, ammunition, and hashish from the Netherlands to Curaçao. Sources in Curaçao reported that the suspects established an elaborate scheme to launder their illicit profits. Among other things, the smugglers purchased property in Curaçao, Colombia, Venezuela, the Dominican Republic, and Lebanon. The Curaçao-based contingent of the drug ring, for instance, operated legitimate businesses on the island that served as front companies for their illicit activities.[142]

Hezbollah has denied any wrongdoing in the Curaçao affair, which is to be expected. In fact, Hezbollah categorically denies involvement in any type of drag trafficking activity. Unfortunately for counterterror and counterdrug authorities, and in spite of several reports allegedly linking Hezbollah to the Curaçao drug trafficking crime ring, no details regarding the exact nature of Hezbollah's involvement have been provided by Curaçao authorities or by the other parties involved in the investigation.[143]

This is not the first time allegations regarding Hezbollah involvement in drug trafficking have failed to be confirmed. In a similar 2008 incident in Colombia, U.S. authorities took down a major drug trafficking ring headed by Lebanese nationals. The suspects were alleged to have channeled part of their funds back to Hezbollah's coffers. However, details explaining the precise Hezbollah link never materialized. In another case in 2005, Colombian and Ecuadorian officials collaborated to expose a Hezbollah-linked global drug trafficking ring. In addition, "According to Ecuadorian officials, the suspects, who included Lebanese, Syrians, Ecuadorians, Colombians, Algerians,

Nigerians, and Turks, are reported to have transferred 70 percent of their profits to Hezbollah."[144] However, as in the previous cases, no concrete details explaining the exact Hezbollah link ever emerged.[145] The authors' best guess for the lack of evidence had more to do with the protection of intelligence assets and confidential sources than claims that Hezbollah was innocent in the affair.[146]

Drug Trafficking Case Study: Saudi-Iranian Plot

In October 2011, the U.S. Justice Department accused Iran of orchestrating a plot to assassinate Abdel al-Jubeir, the Saudi Ambassador to the United States, with a bomb and to also bomb the Saudi and Israeli embassies in Washington, DC. A criminal complaint charged Gholam Shakuri, an officer of the Quds Force, the foreign operations arm of Iran Revolutionary Guard Corps, and Mansour J. Arbabsiar, an Iranian-American and former used-car dealer, with conspiracy to murder a foreign official, to use a weapon of mass destruction, and to commit an act of terrorism. Through intercepted phone calls and bank transfers, officials were able to conclude reports on the alleged terrorist plot pointed to a connection with the Mujahadeen Khalq Organization, a militant group based in Iraq. Shakuri is believed to be an active member of the Iranian opposition group, still designated as a foreign terrorist organization by the U.S. Department of State.[147]

The case began in May, when Arabsiar sought help from a Mexican drug cartel to assassinate the ambassador. The Iranian-American thought he was engaging with a member of the feared Zetas Mexican drug organization, but had unknowingly approached a DEA informant, according to agents. The unwitting Arbabsiar apparently tried to hire the cartel to carry out the assassination in exchange for $1.5 million. Down payments were wired to an undercover bank account, which led to the arrest.[148] The plot demonstrated the threats posed by collaboration between foreign terrorist groups and powerful drug trafficking organizations.

Former Iranian President Mahmoud Ahmadinejad has said he was unaware of any plot, and his spokesman, Ali Akbar Javanfekr, accused the U.S. of fabricating the entire event. U.S. Representative Mike Rogers, chairman of the House Intelligence Committee, was confident the plan was sponsored by top Iranian officials, constituting a clear violation of U.S. and international law, and because of the incident the U.S. Treasury Department imposed further sanctions on Iran.

Drug Trafficking Case Study: Iranians, Turks, and Hezbollah

In a recent case that charged an Iranian and a Turk for supplying weapons and drugs to Hezbollah, prosecutors underscored the growing link between drug trafficking and terrorism. DEA Special Agent Derek Maltz stated, "Drug traffickers and terrorists are joined at the hip in many parts of the world in mutually profitable relationships, and this is one of many examples of that dangerous connection."[149] He announced that Siavosh Henareh and Cetin Aksu were extradited for providing massive amounts of heroin and material support to Hezbollah. The case was uncovered when they attempted to carry out the deal through a DEA agent they believed to be an associate of Hezbollah. The United States Attorney for the Southern District of New York, Preet Bharara, echoed Maltz's position, stating, "This case provides fresh evidence of the growing nexus between drug trafficking, weapons trafficking, and terrorists, a nexus with the potential to threaten our national security."[150]

In June 2010, Henareh began meeting with DEA confidential sources posing as Hezbollah associates in Turkey, Romania, and Greece. During meetings and telephone calls, Henareh agreed to arrange the sale of hundreds of kilograms of high-quality heroin in the U.S. to the DEA undercover operative and was under the assumption that profits would be used to purchase weapons for Hezbollah. Another individual working with Henareh brought a sample of the drug to the DEA operative in Bucharest, Romania, which was to be followed by a multi-hundred kilogram load. Through Henareh, the agent met Aksu and Bachar Wehbe, who agreed to purchase military-grade weaponry on behalf of Hezbollah in Romania, Cyprus, Malaysia, and elsewhere. On 13 June 2011, in Kuala Lumpur, Malaysia, "Aksu and Wehbe signed a written agreement for the purchase of 48 American-made Stinger surface-to-air missiles (SAMs), 100 Igla SAMs, 5,000 AK-47 assault rifles, 1,000 M4 rifles, and 1,000 Glock handguns," for $9.5 million.[151] Wehbe made a $100,000 down payment and indicated that he was purchasing the weapons following requests of Hezbollah. Henareh and Akso were arrested in Bucharest, Romania on 25 July 2011 and Wehbe was arrested in the Republic of the Maldives, and eventually faced the same charges.[152]

This case is a recent example of how terrorist and criminal collusion was successfully identified, investigated, and prosecuted. The undercover operators were able to penetrate trafficking networks that led them to uncover important financial resources for Hezbollah.

Drug Trafficking Case Study: PKK

The Kurdish Communities Union (KCK) and its armed wing, the PKK, have been known to use profits from drug trafficking to fund their extremist activities. Given the widespread dealings with both arms and drug trafficking, as well as arson, blackmail, and extortion, the PKK provides a good nexus case study. Founded as an insurgent group and composed mostly of Kurds living in Turkey, the PKK was launched in 1974 with a goal of establishing an autonomous Kurdish state in southeastern Turkey. The group's objective and activities, however, have shifted, as has its categorization as a major terrorist threat,[153] due to its increased use of terrorism tactics and threats of violence against civilian and military targets.

The magnitude of narcotics operations run by the PKK has grown into what many describe as a monopoly on the drug trade.[154] Turkey is a geographically ideal transshipment point linking Asia and Europe. The PKK dominates the routes through Turkey and Europe and is largely responsible for bringing buyers and sellers together. Germany's chief prosecutor asserted that 80 percent of narcotics seized in Europe have links to the PKK or "other Turkish groups," which often use the profits from illegal narcotics for the purchase of weapons.[155] After experiencing trouble financing its activities, the organization increased production at plantations. For example, there are known opium and cannabis plantations in Osmaniye and Hatay, in mountain villages, and in Lice (Diyarbakır) and other rural areas of Hakkari and Van in Turkey.[156]

In November 2011, a seizure of 28 million Turkish Lira worth of drugs illustrates the tight association and organizational structure of the PKK. Drug production and trafficking are clearly a major financial resource for the organization. In the largest known operation of the PKK/KCK drug business, 44 tons of marijuana was seized in early November.[157]

The PKK works closely with various Kurdish clans and relies heavily on individual couriers in narcotics trafficking to mask its direct involvement. Since those captured generally testify that they are independent businessmen acting alone, it becomes difficult to trace the connection to other criminal or terrorist organizations. Recent arrests, however, have provided information that many are, in fact, KCK/PKK members or militants.[158]

Drug Trafficking Case Study: al-Qaeda in the Islamic Maghreb

While al-Qaeda "central" may not be involved directly in the illicit drug business, increasing evidence links its "well-armed, well-connected" surrogate, al-Qaeda in the Islamic Maghreb (AQIM), to drug trafficking operations in North and West Africa.[159] Some contend that AQIM does not use narcotics due to religious reasons and only provides "security" for traffickers as they move product through West and North Africa to lucrative markets in Europe.[160] Others contend that AQIM is aggressively pursuing the drug trade.[161] According to those sources, not only does AQIM offer security for traffickers in the region, it also taxes the shipments and provides geographical guidance and transport protection. Recent evidence affirms that AQIM takes advantage of its local knowledge and connections to move illicit drug products: "The lack of strong state authority and the importance of personal, tribal and ethnic loyalties make it easier to corrupt officials, a fundamental step to guaranteeing the passage of cocaine."[162] Indeed, AQIM operators, along with local, small, affiliated groups—not necessarily Islamists—use their knowledge of the harsh Sahel/Sahara region to guide shipments of drugs. AQIM protects the drug shipments and provides vehicles to transport them to Morocco, then on to Spain, the main entry and distribution point for cocaine in Europe.[163] In the past, AQIM was mainly focused on Algeria, but it is now actively recruiting from other North and West African countries, which makes it easier for the organization to conduct criminal activities in the entire Sahel region.[164]

In a sting operation on 18 December 2010, the DEA arrested three AQIM members from Mali on drug trafficking charges. It was the first time the DEA uncovered an apparently solid connection between Latin American drug smugglers and a well-established terrorist organization with connections to al-Qaeda.[165] During the successful operation, DEA confidential sources posing as FARC agents uncovered a Latin America-Africa nexus between drug trafficking organizations and al-Qaeda that a former DEA official called the "tip of the iceberg."[166]

This operation marked the third time the DEA used confidential sources posing as FARC operators to lure suspected transnational criminals. The first time this tactic had been used, it led to the "capture, arrest and conviction of Syrian arms trafficker Monzer al-Kassar, who was arrested in Spain in 2007."[167] In 2008, a second FARC sting captured arms trafficker Viktor Bout.

Contraband Trafficking

Contraband crimes involve illegally obtained items that evade regulation or taxation, as well as legitimate products that are restricted or taxed differently in the target market than in the home market. High-tax markets have bred the diversion of goods by organized criminal groups.[168] According to ICE, contraband smuggling methods "include the use of high-speed vessels, cargo containers, aircraft, commercial trucking, commercial vessel, and human carriers."[169] Large-scale contraband crimes could include product piracy, cargo crime, smuggling, hijacking, or tax evasion. The most commonly smuggled goods involved in tax evasion crimes are rare stones and cigarettes.

U.S. lawmakers have made attempts to strengthen legislation deterring cigarette trafficking, such as the Prevent All Cigarette Trafficking Act (H.R. 1676), which was passed by the U.S. House of Representatives on 21 May 2009. The Senate Judiciary Committee amended and submitted a similar bill, which was passed by the Senate on 11 March 2010 and by the House a week later.[170] The Bureau of Alcohol, Tobacco, Firearms, and Explosives (ATF) has primary jurisdiction over criminal provisions related to tobacco in the Contraband Cigarette Trafficking Act of 1978. H.R. 1676 would allow ATF to establish tobacco trafficking teams, an intelligence center, a covert national warehouse for undercover operations, and a computer database to track the illegal transactions involving tobacco products.[171] Contraband is often accorded relatively low priority from law enforcement, and it is viewed as a less violent crime than possession of firearms. That said, the ATF has determined that terrorist groups do engage in tobacco diversion and ally with tobacco traffickers to fund their activities.[172]

The varying levels of taxation create incentives for illicit trade and profit in goods such as cigarettes. Because taxes and fees make up a significant portion of final prices (averaging 53 percent), this type of transaction has become a new cash cow for many criminal organizations. According to law enforcement officials, another incentive in the cigarette industry is that illicit tobacco penalties are less severe than those for other forms of illicit trade.[173] Tax increases, display bans, or plain packaging initiatives may in fact benefit the black market.

Contraband and Terrorism

The illicit use of a legitimately produced commodity provides an often over-looked means of terrorist funding. This type of financing activity receives less attention because so little is known about how criminals and terrorists operate in tandem to profit from contraband transactions. It is commonly agreed that natural resources such as diamonds and oil have exacerbated conflict and are exploited for terrorism funding. The trade in manufactured commodities, such as cigarettes or electronic equipment, could be a useful area to further assess.[174] The UN has estimated that 25 percent of the world-wide cigarette trade profits go toward the illicit market, and in 2003 the ATF issued a statement that terrorist organizations increasingly profit from the cigarette black market, which provides a steady flow of income.[175] According to the U.S. Government Accountability Office, the cigarette trade is among the top methods of terrorist fundraising. Participant groups include Hezbol-lah, Hamas, al-Qaeda, Irish Republican Army, PKK, and both the Egyptian and Palestinian Islamic Jihad.[176] According to Louise Shelley, a transnational crime expert at George Mason University and an illicit trade adviser to the World Economic Forum, "terrorist financing through cigarette smuggling is huge," but "no one thinks cigarette smuggling is too serious, so law enforce-ment doesn't spend resources to go after it."[177]

From data gathered on weapons trafficking and explosives accountability, investigators have determined that terrorist organizations may be shifting to tobacco and alcohol commodities to fund their activities.[178] The most traf-ficked contraband items in the world are cigarettes. They are a legal product but are priced or taxed at a level that enables traffickers to make sizable profits by undercutting state-regulated taxes. As state and the federal governments have raised excise taxes on cigarettes, smuggling has become more lucrative and therefore a more attractive activity for terrorists.[179] Transporting 10 cases of contraband cigarettes from low-tax states to high-tax states, for example, can bring in from $18,000 to $23,000 in profits.[180] The illegal diversion and smuggling of cigarettes in the United States results in significant loss in tax revenue to governments. It is difficult to quantify the precise amount, but estimates point to a loss of roughly $1.75 billion for the U.S. government alone.[181] By undercutting retail and wholesale prices, cigarette smugglers also cause legitimate enterprises to lose lucrative business by flooding the market with cheap cigarettes.[182]

There is evidence that terrorist organizations have indeed formed alliances with tobacco traffickers.[183] Since the President's Executive Order on Terrorism Financing in 2001, the ATF has increased efforts to stem the illegal diversion of alcohol and tobacco products that finance criminal and terrorist operations. Since 9/11, 223 cigarette smuggling cases were investigated to locate associations with terrorist groups and their supporters.[184]

Contraband should be viewed as another potential dimension of the nexus, as it provides the same benefits to terrorists as human, weapons, and drug trafficking. Authorities should expand their scope by tracing the intersection between terrorist groups and contraband trafficking in the same way they have with other illicit activity. While it has been difficult to identify direct links between terrorist financing and contraband trafficking profits, law enforcement can make many inferences using the same methods as in other criminal areas. As with human, weapons, and drug trafficking, the approach to identifying the potential overlap between contraband trafficking and terrorist groups is by first cutting off financing sources through the prosecution of individual cases. Of course, individuals engaging in contraband smuggling will likely be found guilty of a range of other criminal violations. Although effective prosecution is impeded by the compartmentalized nature of the investigations (each crime is treated separately), at a minimum, identifying terrorists' involvement in this area of crime will help to further uncover the nexus between criminals and terrorists.

> *Contraband should be viewed as another potential dimension of the nexus, as it provides the same benefits to terrorists as human, weapons, and drug trafficking.*

Contraband Case Study: Charlotte Hezbollah Cell

One way a terrorist organization can benefit from illicit activities such as contraband smuggling is to maintain contacts who have already mastered the black market in a region far from its base. These relationships can serve as a buffer from law enforcement while simultaneously reinforcing sources of funding. Diaspora communities interested in profit for themselves may sympathize with the political motivations of terrorist organizations and send proceeds back to the home country. Hezbollah possesses a vast network of criminal enterprises throughout the world. In 2002, one such North

Carolina-based cell was convicted of providing material support to Hezbollah through contraband profits earned in the U.S.[185] The case of Mohamad Youssef Hammoud illustrates how such a remittance system is carried out and how illicit profits are laundered and set aside to benefit a designated terrorist organization.

After illegally obtaining residency status in the U.S., several aliases, and multiple forms of credit (to facilitate purchasing and transferring of profits), a group based in Charlotte, North Carolina succeeded in transporting cigarettes from the low-tax state of North Carolina to the high-tax state of Michigan.[186] In 2002, the price differential in taxes per carton increased from $7 to $12—translating into a $10,000 profit for the transfer of 1,500 cartons of cigarettes.[187] Investigations uncovered that Mohamad and his brother, Chawki Hammoud, led a group of 12 members in purchasing nearly $8 million worth of cigarettes, earning upwards of $1.5 million. They carried out the operations through complex financial transactions. Purchases were primarily made in cash from the wholesaler J.R. Tobacco. If credit cards were needed for other expenses, the various identities of each member were to be utilized. Once in Michigan, the cigarettes were generally purchased using cash as well. "Shell businesses" or "front" stores were also created to facilitate the smuggling activities.[188]

The FBI confirmed that Mohamad Hammoud was the leader of a group of Lebanese Shia Muslims in Charlotte. He reportedly discussed Hezbollah operations during group gatherings and regularly screened propaganda videos related to the terrorist organization's activities. During such meetings, Hammoud collected donations for Hezbollah to supplement the cigarette smuggling proceeds.[189] Finally, in 2000 police found Hezbollah military operation propaganda and anti-American speeches, books, and pamphlets in the leader's home. Wiretaps used at trial revealed that Hammoud communicated with Lebanon on near-daily basis and would frequently discuss Hezbollah's military operations and counter-intelligence.[190] Hammoud was found guilty of providing material support to a terrorist organization and was sentenced to 155 years in prison.[191]

In addition to convicting the criminals of cigarette smuggling and providing material support to Hezbollah,[192] the investigation helped clarify how terrorist organizations operate and finance their activities in the U.S. The case not only highlighted illicit trade within a legitimate economy, but also how terrorist cells operate within the corporate world.[193] Twenty-six individuals were arrested and prosecuted for immigration fraud, visa fraud, interstate transportation of stolen property, bank fraud, bribery, money laundering, and racketeering, which successfully disrupted the illegal activity and effectively cut terror-crime links.[194] Tracing their complex financial transactions and operations may help to reveal how other cases of contraband trafficking operate and succeed in cooperating with terrorist organizations. Nearly $1.5 million worth of assets were seized in this case.[195]

Contraband trafficking became an integral structural element to the Charlotte cell operations. The material support the group provided for Hezbollah depended on these criminal proceeds. Other criminal activities carried out by the cell, such as fraud, money laundering, and petty crimes, blurred the lines between traditional crime and terrorism but helped in providing additional paths to prosecution. Finally, the Hammoud case demonstrated increased domestic security threats as the geographic reach of terrorist financing activities spanned several regions within the U.S.

As a footnote to the case, in 2003, Hassan Makki and Mohamad Akhdar, operating out of Dearborn, Michigan, pleaded guilty to trafficking contraband, funneling profits to Hezbollah, and conspiring to violate the Racketeer Influenced and Corrupt Organizations Act. Mohamad Hammoud of the Charlotte cell was the primary supplier of cigarettes for the Michigan-based enterprise. Hassan Nashar, a Lebanese native who later testified against the Hammoud brothers, Makki, and Akhdar, provided support to the group via additional cigarette shipments and counterfeit tax stamps.[196]

Contraband Case Study: R.J .Reynolds Cigarette Smuggling— Iraq and PKK

European governments and officials began investigating American manufacturers suspected of selling cigarettes to traders who resold them into black markets designed to evade taxes. In November 2000 in New York, the European Community (EC) filed a civil action accusing conglomerates Phillip Morris and R.J. Reynolds (RJR) of "an ongoing global scheme to smuggle cigarettes, launder the proceeds of narcotics trafficking, obstruct government oversight of the tobacco industry, fix prices, bribe foreign public officials, and conduct illegal trade with terrorist groups and state sponsors of terrorism."[197] The RJR case revealed the practice of corporate malfeasance and highlighted an intricate cooperation between the legitimate corporate world and terrorists. In 2002, RJR was brought to court for using established smuggling routes, shell corporations, fraudulent documentation, and laundering schemes to move cigarettes over the course of a 10-year period. The lawsuit focused on the company's relationship with the PKK and the smuggling of cigarettes into Iraq, which violated a UN embargo. RJR provided assistance to the PKK and other terrorist groups, profiting from a complicated and mutually beneficial scheme involving cigarette sales.

The trade embargo of 1990 Iraq banned most imports to and exports from Iraq.[198] American tobacco products were among the prohibited items for sale in Iraq. RJR devised mechanisms to sell its product in Iraq, circumventing the embargo via a complex and layered scheme, including false documentation and packaging. The cigarettes were moved into Iraq through Turkey, with the PKK receiving a fee for each container transferred through the Kurdish region. According to EC legal filings against RJR, the cigarette proceeds went to the PKK and terrorist organizations based in Northern Iraq. These funds allegedly supported terrorist activities carried out in Europe. In addition to bolstering the operations of the PKK, this "legitimate" multinational corporation helped to establish smuggling routes in the region, violated a U.S. prohibition against trade with Iraq, and violated a UN embargo.[199] Big tobacco companies boosted sales and gain market share by colluding with organized crime syndicates and terrorists.

The PKK holds a unique position when defending its illegal operations. Members of the terrorist organization often claim that financing benefits the Kurdish cause and is therefore not illegal.[200]

Contraband Case Study: Tri-Border Zone

The tri-border area of South America, where Argentina, Brazil, and Paraguay meet has been notorious for the smuggling of drugs, arms, and humans, as well as a haven for money laundering. It has been a breeding ground for contraband items, from CDs and DVDs to fake designer clothing, accessories, sports shoes, games, and electronics. However, cigarettes mark the world's biggest money maker in the contraband category. Paraguay is a top producer of contraband cigarettes, and activities involving the movement of the goods, particularly through the trade hub in Paraguay, have been difficult to thwart. Pat Heneghan, global head of anti-illicit trade for British American Tobacco (BAT), describes the porous borders that make cigarettes fairly easy to smuggle from low-duty Paraguay to high-duty Argentina and Brazil. The significant source of dirty money from cigarettes is a huge problem, and the multinational found that that 6.3 percent of cigarettes worldwide are illicit products (counterfeit, smuggled or sold on a country's black market).[201] Figures from BAT indicate that around 150 billion cigarettes are manufactured in Paraguay annually. However, the country's citizens only consume around three billion cigarettes per year, and only another estimated three billion leave the country legally. This discrepancy suggests that a large portion of the cigarette production is exported to illicit markets. BAT believes that about 8 percent of all illicit cigarettes smoked in the world originate in Paraguay and are smuggled abroad, initially through the tri-border route.[202]

The tri-border area's significant Arab diaspora, largely Lebanese, has a reputation for illicit activity, which is facilitated by unregulated business practices. The region presents another likely scenario of terrorist-trafficking connections. In recent years, U.S. officials began working with local officials on new programs that would uncover money-laundering rings they believed to be funding Hezbollah and other radical groups. The deputy assistant treasury secretary for terrorist financing and financial crimes believed there was strong evidence of the links.[203] Smuggling and money laundering in the region has undoubtedly been on the rise, but according to federal agents in Paraguay, a lack of resources and technology make it extremely difficult to pursue the network of financial crime and illicit trade. One such Paraguayan agent, Maria Adelaida Vasquez, stated, "The criminals are on the vanguard of technology, and we don't even have access to the Internet in our offices. If we have cellphones, it's because we buy them with our own money."[204] In addition, gathering evidence for investigations is exceedingly difficult, as the community remains isolated and few or no local prosecutors speak Arabic.[205]

In 2004, Assad Ahmad Barakat was charged for sending proceeds to Hezbollah. The prominent businessman is of Lebanese descent but holds Paraguayan citizenship. He was running an import-export company as a front, enabling him to send proceeds from smuggling and counterfeiting operations back to Hezbollah. Investigators estimated that Barakat sent about $6 million to the terrorist organization annually from 1999 to 2003.[206]

The area has been closely monitored by intelligence agencies during the last decade, especially following the 9/11 terrorist attacks. However, the tri-border zone is one of the many regions where cigarette smuggling is difficult to investigate and prosecute. Weak controls, corruption, and geography make this area conducive to illicit activity. Combined with the already strong presence of human, weapon, and drug smuggling and the proven link to terrorist organizations such as Hezbollah, the tri-border zone remains a place of concern.

Contraband Case Study: The "Marlboro Connection"

The 2,000-mile stretch across the Sahara and through the Mediterranean is a route for the most lucrative contraband. Cigarette smugglers move product from the West African coast across North Africa, and further north to Europe, where demand fuels this illegal trade. AQIM is largely in control of the trafficking network. With a strong presence in Europe, the Islamic terrorist group relies heavily on cigarette smuggling to these markets.[207] Officials and scholars have even claimed that the cigarette smuggling activities constitute the number one source of financing. In collaboration with Tuareg nomads, AQIM charges protection fees to those moving this favored commodity across the unpoliced desert region.[208] Cigarettes are moved in shipping containers across the north of Mauritania, often through the town of Zerouate, to Kidal in Mali. They are then loaded into smaller trucks for transport to Algeria and eventually Europe. The product enters untaxed through Italy. Journalist Kate Willson claims that cigarette smuggling "has provided the bulk of financing for AQIM. Lead smuggler in the Sahara Mokhtar Belmokhtar was nicknamed 'Mister Marlboro' for his involvement using cigarette smuggling profits to buy weapons."[209] AQIM has weakened governance in this region through its illegal activity. The wave of protests and political upheaval in neighboring countries will create an opportunity for the organization to gain a foothold.[210]

Cultural Property: The Clandestine Art World

The trade in works of art and cultural property is a dimension of illicit trafficking networks worth mentioning.[211] When examined in a broad context, the evidence for the significance of cultural property to security has indeed been mounting in recent years. While there is much literature on theft of cultural property, particularly by so-called subsistence diggers who are driven by poverty and unemployment, there is little scholarly documentation on terrorist group participation in the illicit antiquities trade. However, the value of economic losses related to activities involving stolen art and cultural property follows closely behind the trafficking in illicit narcotics and arms and has thus warranted some investigation. The illegal trade in antiquities alone—which represents just one component of cultural property—has been valued between $300 million to $6 billion per year.[212] This has led many to believe that local trafficking should not be overlooked as a major security threat and method to fund terrorism.[213] Along with the trade in arms, drugs, and human trafficking, some claim the trade in cultural property ranks as one of the most profitable branches of international organized crime and that it also finances international terror organizations.[214] According to the U.S. National Central Bureau of INTERPOL, "the criminal networks trafficking in the illicit sale of works of art and cultural property are often times the same circles that deal in illegal drugs, arms, and other transactions. It has also been recently confirmed that many insurgent and terrorist groups fund their operations through the sale and trade of stolen works of art and cultural property."[215] Despite these assertions, conclusive connections between terrorism and the illicit trade in cultural property are yet to be substantiated through concrete evidence.

Cultural Property Case Study: Iraq

Following the invasion of Baghdad by American and Coalition forces in 2003, the Iraq Museum was devastatingly plundered in a highly publicized looting. The Iraq case provides an example of how chaotic circumstances permitted looting to occur, and suggests that resulting profits fell into the hands of terrorists. It also serves as a reminder to the international community that increased monitoring and protection during vulnerable moments of lawlessness is imperative.

Iraq shares borders with Turkey, Iran, Jordan, Saudi Arabia, and Syria. It is relatively easy to transport materials from Turkey directly to Europe, and from Saudi Arabia to the Gulf States and Europe. There is no precise proof of how or where looted material moves out of Iraq, but it is well known that the recent wars in the country were followed by the establishment of illicit trade networks, which identified key transport routes and mastered effective smuggling techniques.[216]

While serving in counterterrorism operations in Iraq in 2003, Colonel Matthew Bogdanos volunteered to investigate the looting of Iraq's National Museum with a multi-agency task force. Initial investigations estimated that

170,000 artifacts were carried away by looters within 48 hours of the invasion.[217] Approximately 15,000 artifacts were later confirmed stolen and 6,000 priceless objects were recovered following months of raids, seizures, and amnesty programs by the time the museum reopened in 2009. The government has also been buying back artifacts from smugglers.[218] UN Secretary General Kofi Annan issued a statement "deploring the catastrophic losses."[219] Roughly 695 artifacts from the museum were seized in the United States and United Kingdom, and approximately 700 were found by Jordanian, Syrian, Kuwaiti, and Saudi border officials.[220] Other treasures were seized from international antiquities markets in Lebanon and Saudi Arabia.[221]

After conducting an in-depth investigation, Bogdanos explained, "the illegal antiquities trade has become a revenue stream for terrorist activity in the region."[222] He justified this statement through his discoveries that each weapons shipment seized from terrorists or insurgents also contained antiquities. In a December 2005 raid of a terrorist bunker, the team uncovered automatic weapons, ammunition stockpiles, infrared goggles, and uniforms accompanied by "30 vases, cylinder seals and statuettes that had been stolen from the Iraq Museum."[223] The same routes and infrastructure (which were likely established following the 1991 Gulf War) were used to move the items, whether weapons or artifacts. Bogdanos points out that a place like Iraq, unlike other unstable regions, does not have a huge drug market, so smugglers turn to other markets. He adds, "When you consider the routes out of Iraq and on to the rest of the world ... via Lebanon, it should come as no surprise that Hezbollah saw this movement as a source of financial gain. We began to see Hezbollah taxing the movement of antiquities."[224] Other observers claimed that Sunnis, Shiite militia, and possibly al-Qaeda in Iraq were taking advantage of this lucrative trade in looted antiquities as a funding source. The revenue flowed from a seemingly endless supply of antiquities also helped finance civilian and military attacks.[225] While the information is largely anecdotal, the case does provide useful information for criminal investigations.[226]

2. Challenges and Opportunities

Challenges

Fighting terrorism is difficult; so is battling HWDC-trafficking. Fighting terrorists and traffickers when they are working in tandem is doubly difficult due to a number of operational and legal considerations. Operationally, domestic and international efforts for countering both drug trafficking and terrorist activities are difficult to synergize. Domestically, U.S. counterterror activities are the responsibility of the Department of Justice and its lead agency, the FBI; the Department of Homeland Security; and 87,000 different policing jurisdictions.[227] Internationally, U.S. counterterror responsibilities rest with the Department of State and the DOD. Domestically, counter-drug activities are also the responsibility of the Department of Justice—but the lead agency is the DEA, not the FBI—and 87,000 different policing jurisdictions. The Department of Homeland Security and several of its agencies—ICE,[228] the Coast Guard,[229] and the Department of Customs and Border Protection[230]—have supporting counterdrug responsibilities that mostly entail keeping drug traffickers out of the country. Internationally, drug trafficking is the responsibility of the Department of State, with the DOD in a supporting role.[231]

Therefore, a disparate number of federal, state, county, and local organizations and law enforcement agencies are responsible for countering terrorist and/or drug trafficking organizations that operate in a broad geographical area. Unfortunately, neither terrorists nor traffickers recognize borders or boundaries—international or domestic—which exacerbates the ability of the myriad of agencies bound by jurisdiction requirements to "connect the dots."

Legally, terrorism is handled as a national security issue, while drug trafficking is not—which makes little sense, considering that illicit drug activity kills more Americans every year than terrorism. According to testimony given before the U.S. House of Representatives, "More than 31,000 Americans—or approximately ten times the number of people killed by terrorists on 11 September 2001—die each year as a direct result of drug abuse."[232] Some are trying to "elevate" illicit drug activity to the same national security status as terrorism. For example, Texas congressman Michael McCaul, a Republican from Austin, is seeking to designate seven of the top Mexican cartels as "foreign terrorist organizations" (FTOs), a move he says would give law enforcement in the United States enhanced tools to combat the drug cartels. Currently, leaders of drug cartels reside in what they consider to be safe havens—areas where they cannot be pursued by the criminal justice system.[233] Phil Jordan, the former El Paso Intelligence Center (EPIC) director who also led the inter-agency anti-drug cartel task force EPIC and ran the Dallas Drug Enforcement Agency office, explained that drug cartel members break the law on the Mexican side of the border because they know they get away with it; solving the cases then becomes extremely difficult for American authorities. Jordan advocates labeling some cartels meeting specific criteria as terrorist organizations to be a potential way to improve security.[234]

Why not broaden the reach of law enforcement so that violent crime can be appropriately prosecuted? Legislation proposed by McCaul in H.R. 1270 (March 2011) would permit the government to freeze money tied to the trafficking organizations and enhance the criminal penalties for those found aiding the cartels, much in the same manner as the law is used against al-Qaeda and other terrorist groups.[235] Penalties, including large fines and prison sentences, would apply to the entire organization, not only the leaders. Placing the Mexican drug cartels—and perhaps other cartels as well—on FTO list would also give law enforcement officers the authority to limit travel operations and deport any cartel member involved.[236] In a letter dated 27 April 2011, representatives Mike Rogers, Jeff Duncan, Dan Burton, Sue Myrick, and Brian Bilbray urged Secretary of State Hillary Clinton to support the designation of certain Mexican drug cartels as terrorist organizations and to "develop a comprehensive strategy to assist the Mexican government win the war against the cartels."[237] McCaul explains that the violence toward the Mexican government, legal system, and media threatens the very foundation of that nation and that the Obama administration requires tools to ensure security at the border. The new strategy is intended to create communication channels among involved agencies and to implement new technologies and plans to coordinate efforts between the Justice Department and Treasury Department's Office of Foreign Assets Control.[238] By labeling the cartels as terrorist organizations, the task of targeting the criminal activities will be simplified and prosecution will be made more effective.

The money trail left behind by both criminal and terrorist organizations will be one of the most promising ways to identify the growing nexus between them and will be an effective means of deterring activity. Several of the case studies outlined in this paper demonstrate how following transactions between bank accounts helped investigators to pinpoint the associations and make appropriate arrests. A powerful way to topple the nexus would be to dry up its financial sources. U.S. Treasury officials have worked with the Department of Homeland Security's immigration office to help local officials in high-risk regions, such as the South American tri-border zone. Involvement in the banking sector is encouraged to reduce money laundering. The United States is equipping foreign governments with the means to implement "trade-transparency units."[239] This is a way to collect and analyze trade data in an effort to uncover irregularities that could help destabilize terrorist-trafficking activity. These tactics are less-cited examples of how to stem the trafficking that finances terrorists, but are undoubtedly an important means of controlling the illicit flow of goods, particularly weapons or weapons technology.

Opportunities

While targeting and disrupting the trafficking-terrorist nexus is replete with challenges, the nexus also creates several opportunities for its exploitation. First, tracking terrorists for their illicit activities, rather than their terrorism-based endeavors, is less complicated. One of the reasons law enforcement agencies were successful against terrorist groups such as the Baader Meinhof Gang and the Red Army Faction (RAF) in the 1960s was because law enforcement agencies and the legal system adapted to more easily target these "criminal activities." In 1976, West Germany increased police powers to deal with terrorism and made it a crime to establish a terrorist organization.[240] Further,

> ... tracking terrorists for their illicit activities, rather than their terrorism-based endeavors, is less complicated.

the establishment of an anti-terrorism paramilitary unit proved invaluable. The Federal Republic of Germany's "formidable computerised [sic] bank of counterterrorism data," and establishment of *Grenzschutzgruppe 9*—Border Protection Group 9 "helped the West German police capture some of the key members of the RAF who were on the run."[241] These centralized police responses to the criminality of the terrorist activities enabled them to be "successful overall in the quelling of the RAF."[242]

Second, while some nations might not be willing to acknowledge a terrorism problem within their borders, they are more likely to acknowledge a criminal problem. This example is highlighted by the case of Hezbollah in the tri-border area of Argentina, Paraguay, and Brazil. In December 2006, the U.S. Treasury Department's designation of certain Lebanese expatriates in the area as having ties to Hezbollah spurred the governments of Argentina, Brazil, and Paraguay to issue a "joint statement exculpating the suspects and rejecting U.S. claims about terrorist activity in the region."[243] However, the State Department's 2007 annual report on terrorism "reveals that these three governments take a markedly more aggressive approach to other criminal activities."[244] The report states that the three nations "have long been concerned with arms and drugs smuggling, document fraud, money laundering, and the manufacture and movement of contraband goods through this region."[245] While these governments might not be willing to publicly support U.S. counterterrorism policy, their enforcement of existing laws is both internationally and domestically acceptable and would still further shared goals of targeting the nexus.

Third, the counter-criminal approach is appealing because it can leverage existing resources and procedures. The approach:

> ... requires neither changes to domestic legal structures nor a reorganization of government bodies or legal, administrative, and regulatory authorities. Drug laws are comprehensive and ubiquitous; governments must simply enforce existing laws and hold terrorists accountable for their criminal transgressions. Enforcing domestic laws is not a political statement, but merely a function of law and order and of national sovereignty.[246]

This relates not only to the ease of operations within a legal framework, but also to the second point about some nations' reluctance to openly discuss or act against terrorism. While "some countries use the rhetoric of counter-terrorist cooperation but are unwilling to shoulder their responsibilities in practice, such as restricting the travel of terrorists through their territory or ratifying United Nations conventions on terrorism,"[247] many nations are more willing to act against crimes codified in their own legal codes.

Fourth, it is easier to prosecute terrorists for criminal activity than for crimes of terrorism.[248] Indeed, collecting solid evidence about terrorism may be more difficult than collecting evidence for many drug, immigration, and white collar crimes.[249] In terrorism-related procedures, evidence often comes from intelligence sources, which can pose significant evidentiary challenges in court. In fact, the evidence may be inadmissible because its use may compromise valuable sources or methods, "or the evidence may have been supplied by a foreign government unwilling to publicly acknowledge its cooperation with the United States."[250] Evidence in criminal prosecution faces far fewer constraints. For example, many criminal charges actually brought under the international and domestic terrorism programs do not involve violent acts or even the threat of violence. The most frequent, in fact, appear to reflect technical violations including false statements on visas, identification records such as drivers' licenses, or other documents.[251]

Fifth, disclosing terrorists' criminal activities has positive public relations implications. Exposing terrorists for what they are—criminals—sullies their "freedom fighter" or pious religious images and inhibits their opportunity to raise funds and recruit. The Federal Narco-Terrorism statute of 2006 has already been used in several cases and will likely play an increasingly important role in terms of enforcement and highlighting "terrorist groups' hypocritical involvement in criminal activity."[252] This type of public relations campaign can help support grassroots movements to discredit terrorist and criminal causes and provide much-needed assistance to governmental efforts to disrupt these types of activities. There may well be other silver linings to the nexus challenge as well. For instance, penetrating terrorist organizations, particularly Islamist extremist organizations such as al-Qaeda, is difficult—if not impossible. Indeed, religious extremists are more difficult to infiltrate than terrorists of previous generations. The networked, cellular structure used by al-Qaeda and like-minded groups is particularly difficult to navigate for a hierarchical security apparatus like that of the United States. While bribery and other traps could yield information and prosecutions for traditional criminal groups in the past, the $50 million reward on Osama bin Laden was never collected. And, despite bin Laden's recent killing, it is still unclear how successful other methods have been in getting bin Laden's followers to talk.[253] Therefore, one potentially successful strategy would be to employ undercover operators to actively penetrate trafficking organizations known to be linked to terrorist entities, with the goal of getting close enough to the group to collect actionable intelligence. Alternatively, arrested traffickers with known terrorist associations should be convinced to share their knowledge of those terrorist organizations with intelligence and law enforcement officials.[254]

Seeking the cooperation of unsavory criminal elements during conflict is not new. Many credit Mafia kingpin Lucky Luciano for aiding Naval Intelligence during World War II: "In return for reduction in his prison sentence in 1942, it is often speculated that Luciano made a deal with the U.S. government to secure New York's docks from Nazi or Fascist sabotage and to provide human intelligence that would be used during the invasion of Sicily."[255] Interestingly, during the invasion of Sicily in July 1943—possibly because of Luciano's connections and influence—Italian troops did not fire a single shot at the invading Americans.[256] How might a "Lucky Luciano" arrangement work today? Consider weapons trafficker Viktor Bout, who is presently languishing in a U.S. prison on weapons trafficking and terrorism charges. Bout purportedly had dealings with al-Qaeda,[257] Hezbollah,[258] and Abu Sayyaf,[259] among other terrorist groups. Someone like Bout would be a prime candidate to take the offer of a reduced sentence in exchange for valuable information about his former associates.[260]

As discussed, one way to anticipate areas of converging criminal and terrorist interest is to identify ungoverned or loosely governed geographical locations where both terrorist and criminal activity are likely to proliferate. This "failed states" approach may be effective in some cases by providing an approximation of a country's stability or likelihood of collapse. However, by focusing on the "failed states" approach, places like Abbottabad, Pakistan, where Osama Bin Laden was killed, can go unnoticed by international analysts.[261] The Global Black Spots-Mapping Global Insecurity (GBS-MGI) Program is currently developing a way to target terrorists through what has been called the "Black Spots" approach, which has three dimensions. A "Black Spot" will be outside of governmental control; it will be dominated by illicit organizations; and it will be able to produce and export insecurity (i.e., the organizations possess explosives, illicit drugs, and other instructions within terrorist networks).[262] Not only does Pakistan have a strong military and considerable nuclear weapons, it has a strong intelligence apparatus. Here, the GBS-MGI approach allows for a more intricate analysis of provinces, cities, and districts and the presence

A "Black Spot" will be outside of governmental control; it will be dominated by illicit organizations; and it will be able to produce and export insecurity …

of warlords, crime organizations, insurgent groups, and terrorist networks.[263] A causal model for identifying these critical nodes in terrorist and other extremist networks can link Black Spots to capture the likelihood of collaboration through the use of technology and other investigative techniques targeted and exploited by law enforcement and technology. To date, GBS-MGI has identified 600 Black Spots worldwide.[264]

While there are certainly challenges presented by the collusion and outright collaboration of terrorist and criminal groups, these relationships have the potential to provide openings for governments to infiltrate, intercept, and prosecute traditionally hard-to-access terrorist groups. In fact, the terror-crime nexus presents interesting opportunities—perhaps even advantages—for counterterrorism and anticrime officials to consider.

Conclusion

Recent evidence suggests increasing and deepening connections between HWDC-trafficking and terrorism, thought the two were previously considered mutually exclusive. The lines between criminal trafficking and terrorist organizations are increasingly blurred—in large part as a result of the similarities between the two phenomena. Trafficking and terrorist groups have a natural affinity with one another due to their engagement in illicit activities and their use of violence, fear, and corruption to attain their goals. They operate clandestinely in denied areas that stretch across the globe, where governmental controls are weak. Still, there are differences between trafficking organizations and terrorist groups. While criminal organizations focus on creating profits through illicit means, terrorist groups have goals that stretch beyond pure wealth creation. Terrorists, altruists in their own eyes, have ideological goals, serve a specific constituency, and use terrorist tactics to attain their objectives. While differences persist, criminal and terrorist groups have learned from one another, selecting activities to further their objectives such as using IEDs or laundering money.

The "big four"—human, weapons, drug, and contraband trafficking—are connected to terrorism in a variety of ways. Although the links between human traffickers and terrorist groups are the least established among the big four, suggested relationships in Africa and the former Soviet Union States are becoming more frequent. Weapons traffickers, in contrast, are much more connected to terrorism and terrorist groups. Having a natural affinity to armed conflict, weapons traffickers are often connected to armed groups and harbor nefarious intentions. Weapons traffickers rely on terrorists for protection, and terrorists rely on weapons traffickers for weapons—it is a naturally symbiotic relationship, particularly when both can profit from the enterprise.

Drug profits are important, particularly for terrorists such as al-Qaeda and Hezbollah, whose other funding sources are drying up. Therefore, the links between drug traffickers and terrorists are primarily focused on generating income, and to a lesser extent on creating or fueling violence and conflict. Yet the links between drug trafficking and terrorism are the most entrenched and fastest-growing of all three forms of trafficking illustrated here. The relationship varies across a spectrum, from straightforward "marriages of convenience" between drug traffickers and Islamist extremists to a true "nexus," as in the case of the FARC, the world's first narco-terrorist group.

Recognizing that there is a nexus between certain trafficking and terrorist organizations is an important first step in successfully addressing and combating each type of group. Recognizing that law enforcement and counterterrorist officials might have an opportunity to use their abilities to penetrate criminal organizations in order to gain access to terrorist groups is perhaps even more important. Since it is easier to infiltrate criminal organizations, it may therefore be easier to gain access to terrorist organizations that have criminal associations. Nevertheless, challenges to counter-trafficking and counterterrorist operations persist. From a legal standpoint, counterterrorist laws are more comprehensive than their counter-drug counterparts. The ongoing effort to raise drug trafficking to the same national security level as terrorism is a positive sign. We have much to learn from the collusion of trafficking and terror. Recognizing the similarities, differences, and areas of cooperation between these two dangerous types of organizations will ensure that counter-trafficking and counterterrorist activities are more focused and ultimately more successful.

Finally, the policy challenges to combating a crime-terror nexus are numerous, and affect a wide variety of governmental institutions with responsibilities to combat either crime or terror.[265] Many of the institutions involved in the fight against the crime-terror nexus, including the departments of State, Treasury, Defense, Justice, and Homeland Security, as well as the intelligence community, suffer from separation of the offices that handle crime and terror. The U.S. Department of State, for example, has separate units that handle counterterrorism efforts (the Office of the

Coordinator for Counterterrorism) and combat international organized crime (the Bureau of International Narcotics and Law Enforcement Affairs). Since 9/11, however, these units have learned to work together, creating complementary programming that often has the same end goals. Unfortunately, the examples of such cooperation across government are not as prevalent. Therefore, to address terrorist-trafficker nexus challenges in the future, officials must foster

> ... to address terrorist-trafficker nexus challenges in the future, officials must foster better policy nexus connections between offices with responsibilities for countering terrorism and combating international crime.

better "policy nexus" connections between offices with responsibilities for countering terrorism and combating international crime. What is required is a nimble organizational structure that would combat terror-crime nexus challenges with a "policy nexus" that works.

3. The Terrorist-Trafficking Nexus and Special Operations Forces

Introduction

Special Operations Forces (SOF) have been engaged in counterterror operations and counter-drug trafficking, or counter-narcotics operations, for decades. Operation Snow Cap in South America in the late 1980s partnered United States Special Operations Forces (USSOF) and DEA teams to conduct counter-narcotics operations. The joint teams "provided paramilitary training, law enforcement planning, intelligence and advisory support for counterdrug raids on cocaine processing labs and airstrips in Bolivia, Peru and Ecuador."[266] In what was the normal method of operation for decades, U.S. military personnel were in a support role and confined to their bases, where they trained host country forces to conduct joint operations with DEA agents.[267]

Presently, SOF continue to support counter-drug operations in South America and are often touted as a positive factor in turning the tide against drug traffickers in all of Latin America.[268] SOF also support counter-drug operations in other combatant commands, particularly in Central Command, as part of the ongoing counterterror and counterinsurgency efforts in Afghanistan. When one of this monograph's authors commanded the 1st Special Forces Group between 1994 and 1996, detachments from his command conducted counter-drug operations in Thailand, supported Joint Task Force Six counter-drug operations on the border of Mexico and, for a brief period, helped monitor drug crossing points on the U.S.-Canada border. These operations were either training or support missions, but they were still integral to the overall U.S. counter-drug strategy.

Specific authorities for investigating and countering terrorism and criminal activities are laid out in the Foreign Assistance Act of 1961 (as amended), Title 10 of the U.S. Code, and various National Defense Authorization Acts.[269] Under Title 10 and authorized missions, SOF clearly have authority to participate in counterterror operations, as do several other federal agencies. However, unlike other federal agencies, SOF's authority to conduct counter-drug trafficking and other counter-trafficking operations is less clear. Agencies that are legally authorized to conduct both counterterror and anti-crime (counter-trafficking) operations include the FBI, DEA, ICE, and the International Organized Crime Intelligence and Operations Center.[270]

FBI

The FBI receives its authority to investigate all federal crime not assigned exclusively to another agency in Title 28, Section 533 of the U.S. Code. It is also authorized to investigate

> … threats to national security pursuant to presidential executive orders, attorney general authorities, and various statutory sources. Title II of the Intelligence Reform and Terrorism Prevention Act of 2004, Public Law 108-458, 118 Stat. 3638, outlines FBI intelligence authorities, as does Executive Order 12333; 50 U.S.C. 401 et seq.; 50 U.S.C. 1801 et seq. On foreign soil, FBI special agents generally do not have the authority to make arrests except in certain cases where, with the consent of the host country, Congress has granted the FBI extraterritorial jurisdiction.[271]

DEA

The DEA receives its authority from Title 21, Chapter 5A of the U.S. Code, which creates the DEA as the one comprehensive agency for the enforcement of drug laws and gives it the authority to enforce the Controlled Substances Act. More importantly, Section 122 of the USA PATRIOT Improvement and Reauthorization Act of 2005 (P.L. 109-177) prohibits narco-terrorism, with provisions for enhanced criminal penalties. Codified in Title 21, Section 960a of the U.S. Code, this language makes it "a violation of U.S. law to engage in narcotics-related crimes anywhere in the world while knowing, conspiring or intending to provide support, directly or indirectly, for a terrorist act or to a terrorist organization."[272] In order to enforce counter-narco-terrorism provisions, the DEA has established the Counter-Narco-Terrorism Operations Center under the umbrella of its Special Operations Division. In cases such as Afghanistan, the DEA carries out operations through Foreign-Deployed Advisory and Support Teams (FAST) that partner with the host country on joint investigations,[273] much the same way that military special operations forces collaborate with their host's counterpoints to carry out similar missions.

ICE

ICE is authorized to investigate smuggling cases under Title 18 – General Smuggling; Title 19 – Customs Duties; and Title 21 – Narcotics Violations.[274] Within ICE, the National Security Investigations Division is responsible for leading the effort to "identify, disrupt and dismantle transnational criminal enterprises and terrorist organizations that threaten the security of the United States."[275]

SOF

As mentioned previously, counterterrorism is a SOF "core operation" as noted in USSOCOM Publication 1, "Doctrine for Special Operations"[276] and as a special activity in Title 10 U.S. Code Chapter 6.[277] However, SOF have no counter-trafficking law enforcement authority under existing statutes. U.S. law enforcement bodies are clearly authorized to conduct international counter-trafficking operations, particularly counter-drug trafficking. But not granting SOF these authorities in an international environment may be short-sighted. For example, the security environment of a host nation may be non-permissive to the investigatory and prosecutorial missions of these agencies. When a host nation's forces are ill equipped to conduct counter-terrorism and/or anti-trafficking operations, or the security environment prevents U.S. law enforcement agencies from operating effectively, the U.S. military, specifically SOF, is ideal for contributing to "joint counternarcotics and counterterrorism or counterinsurgency activities."[278]

In fact, until recently, SOF support for countering human, weapons, and contraband trafficking has been limited. Other than support for counter-drug operations, SOF involvement in these efforts has been mostly coincidental—a side effect of other counterterror or counter-drug operations.[279] While counterterror is a SOF core operation, as previously noted, there is little specificity regarding SOF and counter-drug operations. Interestingly, counter-drug operations—once listed as a collateral mission in SOF doctrine[280] —are not mentioned as a mission, operation or activity in USSOCOM Publication 1.[281] However, in an April 2011 joint publication, SOF are able to "perform other activities of a collateral nature such as counterdrug operations and noncombatant evacuation operations."[282] On the official U.S. Army Special Operations Command website, counter-drug operations are listed as a collateral activity for Special Forces.[283] SOF's participation in counter-drug/

counter-narcotics operations is authorized under Title 10 of the United States Code. For example, Counter Nacro-Terrorism funding was approved to augment already existing Counter Drug/Counter Narcotics authorities to train and advise host nation security forces. This DOD (Title 10) exception enables SOF teams to train and provide direct assistance to friendly foreign forces, and it specifically addresses the nexus of terror and narco-crime organizations.

Other counter-trafficking activities—such as weapons, human, and contraband trafficking—are not listed in SOF-related doctrine or directives as missions, activities or collateral activities. However, if the nexus between terrorists and traffickers becomes more pronounced and threatening to the United States (a clear and present danger), look for policymakers to suggest SOF become more involved in counter-nexus type operations—whether willingly or unwillingly.[284]

Counter-Drug Trafficking

In truth, SOF are presently engaged in counter-nexus-type operations—and have been for decades. For example, operations against the FARC by definition have both counterterror and counter-drug implications. The FARC is as much engaged in trafficking cocaine today as it is in leftist terrorist activities to affect regime change in Colombia.[285] Similarly, SOF are engaged in operations against the Taliban, another narco-trafficking organization. In fact, Mario Costa, the former UN Drug Czar, described the Taliban's heroin trade in Afghanistan and Pakistan as the "new clear and present danger."[286] As in role in South American counter-drug operations, SOF generally plays a support role in Afghanistan. Ideally, Afghan units, including the Afghan Ministry of Interior's Air Interdiction Unit (AIU), will take full responsibility for the counter-drug mission in the near future. The AIU met a major milestone in August 2011 by conducting an integrated counter-drug operation with the Afghan National Intelligence Unit, Afghan commando forces and allied coalition advisers. According to AIU officials, the mission originated "from the Afghan Air Force compound in Kabul, was flown by Afghan AIU Special Forces pilots" and destroyed illegal drugs and drug-making equipment in Achin District in Nangahar province.[287]

The extent to which SOF are committed to counter-drug operations in Afghanistan is beyond the scope of this work. However, a comment made by Michael Braun, former Chief of Operations for the DEA, perhaps best sums up SOF participation in counter-drug operations and telegraphs a recommendation forthcoming in this monograph. According to Braun, as of October 2009, almost all counter-narcotics operations in Afghanistan were executed with "U.S. Military Special Forces operators working shoulder-to-shoulder with law enforcement agents."[288] He added, "When you fuse the unparalleled tradecraft that seasoned DEA agents bring to the fight with the exclusive war fighting techniques of highly experienced Special Forces operators, you create a counter-insurgency capability that is second-to-none. More of this blend would definitely be better, and would be a wise investment of taxpayer dollars."[289]

Since drug money is used to finance terrorist operations, recruiting, and training, SOF are logically able to assist in counter narco-terrorist operations. This logic was made clear in a 2004 speech delivered by Thomas O'Connell, then the Assistant Secretary of Defense for Special Operations and Low Intensity Conflict, before a Senate Armed Services Committee hearing. According to Secretary O'Connell:

> Global and regional terrorists threatening United States interests can finance their activities with the proceeds from narcotics trafficking. Terrorist groups such as the FARC in Colombia, Al Qaida in Afghanistan, and groups around the world partially finance key operations with drug money. The DOD, with our counterparts in the Department of State and other government agencies, seeks to systematically dismantle drug trafficking networks, both to halt the flow of drugs into the United States, and to bolster the broader war on terrorism effort.[290]

Other counter-trafficking operations

In Africa, the Pan Sahel Initiative (PSI) was a 2002 U.S. State Department-funded initiative in designed to enhance the border capabilities of Mali, Mauritania, Niger, and Chad in order to prevent arms smuggling, drug trafficking, and the movement of trans-national terrorists. U.S. Army Special Forces, assigned to U.S. European Command's Special Operations Command, Europe, trained selected military units from the four countries on mobility, communications, land navigation, and small unit tactics.[291] Another objective of the PSI was to bring military and civilian officials together to encourage more cooperation and information sharing within and among the governments of the region on counterterrorism and border security issues. Under the PSI, Special Forces soldiers helped train and equip one rapid-reaction company—about 150 soldiers—in each of the four sub-Saharan states.[292] Critics contend that the PSI was both significantly underfunded and lacking focus.[293]

A follow-on program, initially referred to as the Trans-Sahara Counterterrorism Initiative and eventually established under U.S. Africa Command (AFRICOM) as the Trans-Sahara Counterterrorism Partnership (TSCTP), is better funded and has a wider scope, with several countries added to the program. From a SOF perspective, the overall goals of the TSCTP "are to enhance the indigenous capacities of governments in the Pan-Sahel (Mauritania, Mali, Chad, and Niger, as well as Nigeria and Senegal) to confront the challenge posed by terrorist organizations in the region. Additionally, TSCTP facilitates cooperation between the Pan-Sahel countries and Maghreb partners (Morocco, Algeria, and Tunisia) in combating terrorism."[294] The U.S. Department of State's TSCTP goals and objectives are more robust in that they include counter-criminal trafficking operations as well; its primary TSCTP objective is to create an environment in the Maghreb and Trans Sahel that is inhospitable to terrorist and trafficking operations. Commensurate with host country need and political will, the TSCTP program's intent is to place law enforcement experts in requesting countries capable of lending assistance to local law enforcement personnel on a day-to-day basis.[295]

Counter-Human Trafficking

Special Forces soldiers are presently attempting to capture a notorious human trafficker in Central Africa—terrorist Joseph Kony. Deployed by President Barack Obama at the end of 2011, the 100 U.S. Special Forces soldiers dedicated to this mission operate out of four bases and are split up about 15 to 30 per base. Their purpose is to provide American technology and experience to Central African and Ugandan forces in pursuit of Kony and his Lord's Resistance Army (LRA) followers.[296] The Kony-led LRA promotes a radical form of Christianity and African animism, which it claims should be the basis for the Ugandan government.[297] In attempting to achieve its objective, the LRA's tactics have included unbridled brutality, rape, torture, and murder against civilians.[298] Approximately 80 percent of Kony's ranks—or 3,000 human beings—are trafficked children, who were kidnapped and brainwashed into service with the LRA.[299] LRA members also kidnap children, particularly girls, to serve as sex slaves; some have even been trafficked as "gifts" to arms dealers in Sudan.[300]

Counter-Weapons Trafficking

Presently, SOF do not have any particular weapons trafficking authority under Title 10 or in SOF doctrine, nor do they have any dedicated missions or collateral activities. Perhaps they should. According to Special Operations researcher John B. Alexander, the resources of criminal organizations are increasingly posing direct threats to stability, and studies have proven that illegal drug trafficking is the leading funding source for terrorism. However, rather than concentrating on a single vice, transnational organized crime elements span many different facets of activities. Of particular concern is the relationship between trafficking and terrorist organizations.[301]

Case Studies

Beyond the central theatres of war in Iraq and Afghanistan, SOF has conducted similar missions across the globe, denying sanctuary to terrorist/trafficking groups from the Philippines to Honduras.

Africa

According to Colonel George Bristol, commander, Joint Special Operations Task Force-Trans Sahara, Africa is the "next true horizon."[302] It is an expansive and often poorly governed territory where the full spectrum of international powers, African states, and local actors are fighting for scarce natural resources. Such fierce competition for survival perpetuates instability in a region characterized by strong tribal traditions and frequent turnover in governance, allowing trafficking and terrorism to flourish. According to Janice Burton, the nexus where these factors converge is in the exchange of goods, echoing Bristol's observation that "smuggling is considered an honest profession and illicit goods, drugs and weapons are coin of the realm."[303]

SOF have been working with African countries to try and stem the flow of illicit materials and violent ideology through a combination of counter-violent extremist operations and partner-nation capacity building. By taking this two-pronged approach, SOF are able to provide stability in some areas while helping countries spread that stability to their neighbors.

Operation Observant Compass is the deployment of Special Operations Command and Control Element - Horn of Africa, the special operations forces component of AFRICOM's Combined Joint Task Force - Horn of Africa, to counter the Kony-led LRA. A Specially Designated Global Terrorist according to the U.S. Treasury Department, the group has wrought havoc in the countries of Uganda, South Sudan, Democratic Republic of Congo and Central African Republic for nearly three decades. The LRA Disarmament and Northern Uganda Recovery Act was signed into law in May 2010, and in October 2011 President Obama "authorized the deployment of 100 Special Forces advisers to the region, not to engage the LRA, but rather to train the military forces in the region."[304] And according to James Scott Rawlinson, a spokesman for Special Operations Command Africa, American SOF are successfully helping their African partners to pursue the LRA. While he acknowledges that LRA attacks increased slightly in early 2012, he sees that as a sign that the group is feeling pressured and is backed into survival mode. In fact, Ugandan officials believe that the group has split into multiple factions, all of which are constantly on the run and without adequate food.[305] Meanwhile, AQIM poses the greatest threat in North Africa. According to James Kitfield, AQIM has made $90 million over the last decade by kidnapping for ransom and facilitating drug smuggling.[306] AQIM has also been implicated in the 11 September 2012 attack on the American consulate in Benghazi, the January 2013 raid on a natural-gas facility in Algeria, and the seizure of Northern Mali by multiple Islamist groups and Tuareg separatists. In an area also threatened by Boko Haram of Nigeria and al-Qaeda affiliates in Libya, Civil Military Support Elements, Regional Information Support Teams and Special Forces operational detachments have worked closely with partner nations to advise counterterrorism units and limit the territorial control of these groups.

Southeast Asia

In 2002 U.S. Pacific Command initiated Operation Enduring Freedom – Philippines (OEF-P) to counter the growing threat of the al-Qaeda-affiliated Abu Sayyaf Group (ASG) and the Islamist insurgent group Moro Islamic Liberation Front (MILF), both of which operated out of the southern islands of the Philippines. Unlike typical counterterrorism missions, OEF-P:

... focused on assisting the Philippine government to protect its citizens, defeat the Islamist insurgency that had taken hold around the island of Mindanao and the Sulu Archipelago, and deny sanctuary to VENs. OEF-P's success has demonstrated the value of the special warfare approach of working "by, with, and through" partners to achieve common security goals.[307]

While it vacillates between ideological and criminal motivations, ASG has become notorious for its success in kidnappings for ransom, maritime piracy and arms trafficking.[308] With USSOF assistance, Philippine forces won support of the local population and drove ASG from its safe haven on Basilan Island. SOF have continued to train, assist and advise the Armed Forces of the Philippines (AFP) and the Philippine National Police in counterterrorism and counterinsurgency. Renamed Joint Special Operations Task Force-Philippines (JSOTF-P), the SOF presence now consists of 500 to 600 men whose activities are closely coordinated with the ambassador's country team by a full-time SOF liaison officer assigned to the U.S. embassy. This ensures that OEF-P is synchronized with the objectives and activities of U.S. foreign policy toward the Philippines.[309]

JSOTF-P's support for AFP counterterrorism operations is complemented by its civil-military operations which, according to Colonel Bill Coultrup (U.S. Army), a former JSOTF-P commander, "change the conditions that allow those high-value targets to have a safe haven. We do that through helping give a better life to the citizens: good governance, better health care, a higher standard of living ... that's how we prevent the bad guys from getting a grip on the local population."[310]

USSOF and Philippine forces have also driven back the MILF insurgency and disrupted connections between local insurgencies such as MILF and criminal-terrorist groups such as ASG.[311] Moreover, JSOTF-P's supportive role has earned the respect and appreciation of the Philippine government, which recently offered to reopen its bases to conventional U.S. forces.[312] The Philippine government appears eager to cooperate on an expanding set of security challenges, due in no small part to the relationships and trust established by U.S. SOF.[313]

Central America

Members of Naval Special Warfare Task Element-Alpha (NSWTE-A), a deployed maneuver element attached to Naval Special Warfare Unit-FOUR in support of Special Operations Command South, recently trained their Honduran counterparts during a six-month deployment to enhance the abilities of the newly established Honduran Fuerza Especial Naval (FEN). FEN is a Honduran maritime Special Forces unit tasked with combating transnational organized crime in and around Honduras shores. According to the NSWTE-A officer in charge, the partnership has prepared FEN to continue training and operating on its own to protect Honduras borders from transnational organized crime and illicit trafficking.[314]

Conclusion

As previously noted, SOF have been engaged in counter-drug nexus operations for decades in several different regions of the world. Ongoing special operations, such as those in Africa against Joseph Kony and the LRA, may prove successful from a human trafficking perspective. Therefore SOF, at least to a degree, have been and continue to be in counter-trafficking activities in a training and support role—or in a more direct role if the trafficking is specifically related to terrorism activity.

Should SOF have more law enforcement (counter-trafficking) authorities than it does now? The authors believe the answer is yes, particularly in an international environment where transnational, non-state actors operate in denied areas, failed and failing states and along the so-called "arc of instability." John Alexander writes that several emerging factors increase the likelihood that SOF forces and law enforcement agencies will be forced to work together in the future because of the transnational nature of the threat. According to Alexander, the transnational "expansion of international gangs, organized crime organizations and terrorism that has no boundaries and is relegated to criminal status require a coordinated response."[315] He continues,

> Leaving these actions to federal LEAs—such as the FBI, DEA, Secret Service, Alcohol, Tobacco, and Firearms, and others—to solve is insufficient. Rather, area fusion centers that incorporate investigative and response entities at the federal, state, and local levels are already emerging. These amorphous threats have no regard for

geographic limitations. Therefore, our defense mechanisms call for agile, cooperative, and capable confederations that are not hampered by self-imposed limitations.[316]

Military leaders and government officials in the Obama administration have both alluded to the critical role that SOF will play in a U.S. defense strategy increasingly focused on capacity-building and preventative measures. This "light footprint" approach requires a revision of the multiple authorities under which SOF operate in order to effectively address the flexible, amorphous and transnational threat of the terror-trafficking nexus. Specifically, authorities need to support persistent, multi-year engagements rather than episodic training missions. Additionally, existing authorities that restrict U.S. efforts to build partner capacity to the training, advising, and equipping of partner forces that are involved in counterterrorism operations, must be revised or expanded to authorize SOF to engage in a wider mission set.[317]

Endnotes

1. Raven Clabough, "More Drug Arrests Connect Drugs to Terrorism," *The New American*, July 28, 2011. Available at: http://thenewamerican.com/usnews/crime/8385-more-drug-arrests-connect-narcotics-to-terrorism (accessed February 18, 2012).

2. This definition was "coined" by author Russell D. Howard after examining more three dozen terrorism definitions. The Howard definition takes liberties with definitions from Richard Betts and Bruce Hoffman. It is meant to be succinct and useful in analysis. The Howard definition contains three of the most common words or terms in most all recognized definitions: "violence," "civilian," and "for political purposes."

3. Taken from and changes made to: "Prevention of the inadvertent movement and illicit trafficking of radioactive materials," *International Atomic Energy Agency Technical Document 1311*, September 2002, 1. Available at: www-pub.iaea.org/MTCD/publications/PDF/te_1311_web.pdf (accessed February 25, 2012).

4. Multiple conversations with Bruce Hoffman over the past decade.

5. Erick Stakelbeck, "Drug Money Funding Chavez, Islamic Terrorist Groups," Christian Broadcasting Network, November 16, 2010. Available at: www.cbn.com/cbnnews/world/2010/October/Chavez-Drug-Cartels-and-Terrorism-Funding/ (accessed January 11, 2011).

6. John Rollins and Liana Sun Wyler, "International Terrorism and Transnational Crime: Security Threats, U.S. Policy and Considerations for Congress," *Congressional Research Service Report for Congress R41004* (Washington, DC: Congressional Research Service, March 18, 2010, 11. Available at: www.fas.org/sgp/crs/terror/R41004.pdf (accessed April 6, 2012).

7. Multiple conversations and written correspondence between author Howard and Dr. Jeffrey M. Bale over a period of three months, 2011-2012.

8. Ibid.

9. Ibid.

10. "Strategy to Combat Transnational Organized Crime: Addressing Converging Threats to National Security," *National Security Council, Office of the President of the United States*, July 2011, 6. Available at: www.whitehouse.gov/sites/default/files/Strategy_to_Combat_Transnational_Organized_Crime_July_2011.pdf (accessed October 17, 2011).

11. "Remarks for Gen. James L. Jones, National Security Advisor at the Sochi Security Council Gathering, Sochi, Russia," *The White House, Office of the Press Secretary*, October 5, 2010. Available at: www.whitehouse.gov/the-press-office/2010/10/05/remarks-gen-james-l-jones-national-security-advisor-sochi-security-counc (accessed February 26, 2012).

12. Ibid.

13. Two areas where the nexus is highly prevalent are the tri-border area in South America and West Africa. See Horacio Calderon, "Organized Crime and Terrorism in the Triple Border Area," Argentine Center for International Studies, August 24, 2007. Available at: www.horaciocalderon.com/Articulos/HC_TBA_Organised_Crime_and_Terrorism.doc (accessed April 6, 2012). See also Juan Morote Sarion and Thomas Baumert, "Terrorism and Organized Crime: The Economic Nexus," *Universidad Católica de Valencia* Documento de Trabajo No. 8, December 2008, 2. Available at: www.ucv.es/jovellanos/documentos/DT_Jovellanos_8.pdf (accessed April 18, 2011).

14. Louise I. Shelley, "Organized Crime, Terrorism, and Cybercrime." *Security Sector Reform: Institutions, Society and Good Governance*, Alan Bryden and Philipp Fluri, eds. (Nomos Verlagsgesellschaft: Baden-Baden, 2003), 302. See also Frank Shanty, *Organized Crime from Trafficking to Terrorism*, Volume I. September 30, 2007, (ABC-Clio: Santa Barbara) 368.

15. Shelley, "Organized Crime, Terrorism, and Cybercrime," 303.

16. Russell D. Howard, "The Nexus between and among Internationally-Focused Terrorist Groups and Multinational Criminal Cartels" forthcoming.

17. Michael Braun, "Drug Trafficking and Middes East Terrorist Groups, A Growing Nexus," *PolicyWatch #1392 : Special Forum Report*, Washington Institute, July 25, 2008. Available at: http://www.eisf.eu/resources/library/DrugTrafficking-MiddleeastTerrorGroups.pdf (accessed March 2009). See also: Michael Braun, "Regarding The Growing Confluence of Drugs and Terror And the Face of 21st Century Global Organized Crime," Testimony -- Committee on Foreign Affairs, U.S. House of Representatives, October 12, 2011. Available at: http://foreignaffairs.house.gov/112/bra101211.pdf (accessed November 12, 2011).

18. "Anti-Money Laundering/ Combating the Financing of Terrorism: The Fund's Involvement in AML/CFT," International Monetary Fund. Available at: www.imf.org/external/np/leg/amlcft/eng/aml1.htm (accessed April 6, 2012).

19. "Money Laundering and Financial Crimes," International Narcotics Control Strategy Report Volume II, US Department of State, March 2010, 56. Available at: http://www.state.gov/documents/organization/137429.pdf (accessed September 12, 2011).

20. Like the rare 500 euro bill, bin Laden was never seen by most people, hence the nickname.

21. Jonathan Lipow, "Turn in Your bin Ladens," *The New York Times*, December 17, 2010. Available at: www.nytimes.com/2010/12/18/opinion/18lipow.html (accessed April 6, 2012).

22. Samuel Logan, "DEA Uncovers Drug-Terror Nexus," *International Relations and Security Network Security Watch*, January 21, 2010. Available at: http://www.isn.ethz.ch/isn/Current-Affairs/Security-Watch-Archive/Detail/?id=111599&lng=en (accessed April 6, 2012).

23. "Tracking Narco-Terrorist Networks," Security News Center, undated. Available at: http://securityandintelligence.wordpress.com/s-america/ (accessed January 26, 2012).

24. Logan, "DEA Uncovers Drug-Terror Nexus."

25. "Organized Crime Has Globalized and Turned into a Security Threat," United Nations Information Service *UNIS/CP/618*, June 10, 2010. Available at: www.unodc.org/documents/data-and-analysis/tocta/GlobalizationofCrime-PR-Final-English.pdf (accessed May 8, 2011).

26. Bruce Reidel, "Al-Qaeda's tentacles," *The Los Angeles Times*, January 14, 2011. Available at: http://articles.latimes.com/2011/jan/14/opinion/la-oe-0114-riedel-al-qaeda-20110114 (accessed April 24, 2011).

27. Multiple conversations with Dr. Rohan Gunaratna, who keeps tabs on these statistics, as quoted in Russell D. Howard and Margaret J. Nencheck, "The New Terrorism," in Russell D. Howard and Bruce Hoffman, eds., *Terrorism and Counterterrorism: Understanding the New Security Environment*, 4th Edition (Dushkin/McGraw-Hill, 2011).

28. Alex Schmid, "Links between Terrorism and Drug Trafficking: A Case of 'Narco-Terrorism'?" Working Group on Causes of Terrorism, International Summit on Democracy, Terrorism and Security (Madrid, Spain), March 6-11, 2005. Available at: http://english.safe-democracy.org/causes/links-between-terrorism-and-drug-trafficking-a-case-of-narcoterrorism.html (accessed November 1, 2010).

29. Rachel Ehrenfeld, "Drug trafficking, kidnapping fund al-Qaeda," CNN.com, May 3, 2011. Available at: http://articles.cnn.com/2011-05-03/opinion/ehren-feld.al.qaeda.funding_1_islamic-maghreb-drug-trafficking-al-qaeda-central?_s=PM:OPINION (accessed January 7, 2012).

30. "Britain condemns paying ransom to militant groups," Reuters, September 27, 2010. Available at: http://af.reuters.com/article/worldNews/idAFTRE68Q4XE20100927 (accessed January 8, 2012).

31. Joe Kelly, "The business of kidnapping," The Australian, February 17, 2010. Available at: www.theaustralian.com.au/news/features/the-business-of-kidnapping/story-e6frg6z6-1225831111501 (accessed January 8, 2012).

32. Dipak K. Gupta, "Accounting for the Waves of International Terrorism," Perspectives on Terrorism, Vol. 2, No. 11 (November 2008). Available at: www.terrorismanalysts.com/pt/index.php/pot/article/view/55/html (accessed April 6, 2012).

33. Philip Seib and Dana M. Janbek, Global Terrorism and the New Media: The Post-al-Qaeda Generation (New York: Routledge, 2010), 1.

34. Benoit Hervieu, "Organized Crime Muscling in on the Media," Reporters Without Borders Inquiry Report, February 24, 2011. Available at: http://en.rsf.org/IMG/pdf/organized_crime.pdf (accessed January 9, 2012).

35. Alex P. Schmid, "The Links between Transnational Organized Crime and Terrorist Crimes," *Transnational Organized Crime*, Vol.2, No. 4 (Winter 1996): 66-67.

36. Ibid.

37. Bruce Hoffman, Inside Terrorism revised and expanded edition (New York: Columbia University Press, 2006), 62.

38. Alison Jamison, "Transitional Organized Crime: A European Perspective," Studies in Conflict and Terrorism, Volume 24, Issue 5 (September-October 2001), 377-387.

39. Tamara Makarenko, "The Crime-Terror Continuum: Tracing the Interplay between Transnational Organised Crime and Terrorism," Global Crime, Vol. 6, No. 1 (February 2004), 134. Available at: www.silkroadstudies.org/new/docs/publications/Makarenko_GlobalCrime.pdf (accessed January 8, 2012).

40. Ibid.

41. Ibid.

42. Robert Ackerman, "Terrorists and Organized Crime Increase Teaming Efforts, *Signal Online*, March 29, 2012. Available at: http://www.afcea.org/signal/articles/templates/Signal_Article_Template.asp?articleid=2933&zoneid=342 Accessed April 8, 2012. See also: Michael Webster, "Mexican Drug Cartels Using Terrorist Beheading Tactics," Articles Base, April 21, 2008. Available at: www.articlesbase.com/news-and-society-articles/mexican-drug-cartels-using-terrorist-beheading-tactics-392642.html (accessed April 6, 2012).

43. Tim Johnson, "Why are beheadings so popular with Mexico's drug gangs?" McClatchy Newspapers, April 1, 2010. Available at www.mcclatchydc.com/2010/04/01/91481/beheadings-become-signature-of.html (accessed December 31, 2010).

44. David Schwartz and Alex Dobuzinskis, "Police link Arizona beheading to Mexican drug cartel," Reuters, March 3, 2011. Available at: www.reuters.com/article/2011/03/04/us-beheading-arizona-idUSTRE7230L320110304 (accessed April 24, 2011).

45. "Mexican Cartels Using IEDs in Drug Wars," Newsmax.com, December 19, 2010. Available at: www.newsmax.com/InsiderReport/Rubio-Rated-Top-Communicator/2010/12/19/id/380409 (accessed December 13, 2010).

46. Ibid.

47. Ibid.

48. Michael Braun, "Drug Trafficking and Middle Eastern Terrorist Groups: A Growing Nexus?" Washington Institute for Near East Studies *Policy Watch* No.1392: Special Forum Report (July 25, 2008). Available at: www.washingtoninstitute.org/templateC05.php?CID=2914 (accessed January 5, 2011).

49. Lisa C. Carroll, "Alternative Remittance Systems Distinguishing Sub-systems of Ethnic Money Laundering in Interpol Member Countries on the Asian Continent," Interpol, January 1, 2011. Available at: https://www.interpol.int/Public/FinancialCrime/MoneyLaundering/EthnicMoney/default.asp (accessed April 6, 2012).

50. Rollins and Sun Wyler, "International Terrorism and Transnational Crime: Security Threats, U.S. Policy and Considerations for Congress," 11.

51. Charles Bremner and Marie Tourres, "New Threat from al-Qaeda 'Keister Bomb," The Times Online, October 6, 2009.

52. Ibid.

53. As defined by: Stop Trafficking of People (STOP). Available at: http://stoptraf-fickingofpeople.wordpress.com/ (accessed April 15, 2011).

54. "Trafficking in Persons Report 2004," U.S. Department of State Office to Monitor and Combat Trafficking in Persons, June 14, 2004, 14. Available at: www.state. gov/g/tip/rls/tiprpt/2004/34021.htm (accessed April 15, 2011). See also United Nations Office on Drugs and Crime, "Human Trafficking: An Overview," United Nations Global Initiative to Fight Human Trafficking (UNGift), 2008, 7. Available at: www.ungift.org/docs/ungift/pdf/knowledge/ebook.pdf (accessed January 27, 2012).

55. Liana Sun Wyler and Alison Siskin, "Trafficking in Persons: U.S. Policy and Issues for Congress,", Congressional Research Service Report for Congress RL34317 (Washington, DC: Congressional Research Service, 2010), 2. Available at: http:// fpc.state.gov/documents/organization/139278.pdf (accessed April 6, 2012). See also United Nations Office on Drugs and Crime, "Human Trafficking: An Over-view," 7. The UN overview lists the number at 2.5 million.

56. Yuliya Tverdoya, "Human Trafficking in Western Europe: A Comparative Public Opinion Study of Fifteen Nations," University of California at Irvine, August 30, 2011. Available at: http://papers.ssrn.com/sol3/papers.cfm?abstract_id=1919410 accessed April 6, 2012).

57. Beth Simmons and Paulette Lloyd, "Subjective Frames and Rational Choice: Transnational Crime and the Case of Human Trafficking," July 17, 2010. Available at: http://government.arts.cornell.edu/assets/psac/fa10/Simmons_PSAC_Sep10. pdf (accessed January 4, 2012).

58. Justin Bailey, "A Global Survey of International Criminal Entities and Interna-tional Law Enforcement Organizations' Interdiction Again Human Traffick-ing," thesis presented to the Graduate Council of Texas State University-San Marcos, December 2011, 18-21. Available at: http://repositories.tdl.org/txstate-ir/bitstream/handle/10529/ETD-TXSTATE-2011-12-299/BAILEY-THESIS. pdf?sequence=1 (accessed January 4, 2011).

59. Ibid., 18.

60. Russell D. Howard and Colleen M. Traughber, "The 'New Silk Road' of Terror-ism and Organized Crime: The Key to Countering the Terror-Crime Nexus," in Armed Groups: Studies in National Security, Counterterrorism, and Counter Insurgency, Jeffrey H. Norwitz, ed. (Newport, RI: U.S. Naval War College, 2008), 373.

61. Sandra L. Keefer, "Human Trafficking and the Impact on National Security for the United States," Strategy Research Project (Carlisle Barracks, PA: U.S. Army War College, 2006), 3.

62. "Three Plead Guilty to Conspiracy to Provide Material Support to the Paki-stani Taliban," Federal Bureau of Investigation, U.S. Department of Justice, Office

of Public Affairs Press Release, September 12, 2011. Available at www.fbi.gov/miami/press-releases/2011/three-plead-guilty-to-conspiracy-to-provide-material-support-to-the-pakistani-taliban (accessed January 8, 2012).

63. Ibid.

64. Ibid.

65. "Somali Muslim Terrorist in Finland Human Trafficking for Terror Training," *Helsingin Snomat*, November 10, 2011. Available at www.hs.fi/english/article/Police+uncover+suspected+human+trafficking+plan+during+terrorism+investigation/1135269833686 (accessed January 8, 2012).

66. "LTTE arms dealers turn to human trafficking," *Daily News*(Sri Lanka), February 15, 2011. Available at: www.dailynews.lk/2011/02/15/sec00.asp (accessed January 7, 2012).

67. "LTTE Human trafficker arrested at the Katunayake Airport," *Read Sri Lanka*, August 20, 2011. Available at: http://english.readsrilanka.com/2011/08/20/ltte-human-trafficker-arrested-at-the-katunayake-airport/ (accessed January 7, 2012).

68. Raimo Väyrynen, "Illegal Immigration Human Trafficking and Organized Crime," *Discussion Paper No. 2003/72* (Helsinki, Finland: United Nations University/World Institute for Development Economics Research, 2003), 13.

69. Ibid., 13.

70. United Nations Office on Drugs and Crime, "Global human trafficking patterns," July 17, 2003. Available at: www.unodc.org/pdf/speech_2003-07-17_1_slide5.pdf (accessed April 16, 2011).

71. Väyrynen, 1.

72. Yuliya, Tverdova, "Human Trafficking in Western Europe: A Comparative Public Opinion Study of Fifteen Nations."

73. Derek Lutterbeck, "Policing Migration in the Mediterranean," Mediterranean Politics, Vol. 11, No. 1 (March 2006): 63. Available at: http://studium.unict.it/dokeos/2012/courses/1001283C1/document/Lutterbeck-Med_Politics-March06.pdf (accessed April 6, 2012).

74. "13 Arrested in Spain Linked to Terror," *Global Jihad*, February 4, 2009. Available at: www.globaljihad.net/view_news.asp?id=750 (accessed April 17, 2011).

75. Ibid.

76. Bekir Cinar, "Human Trafficking is used for Recruiting Terrorists," Second Annual Interdisciplinary Conference on Human Trafficking, University of Nebraska-Lincoln, October 1, 2010, 9. Available at: http://digitalcommons.unl.edu/cgi/viewcontent.cgi?article=1023&context=humtrafconf2 (accessed February 12, 2012).

77. Ibid., 9-10.

78. Ibid., 11.

79. Ibid., 11-13.

80. Lutterbeck, " Policing Migration in the Mediterranean," 59-82.

81. Ibid., 79.

82. Sinikukka Saari, "Balancing between inclusion and exclusion: The EU's fight against irregular migration and human trafficking from Ukraine, Moldova and Russia," Working Paper (London: London School of Economics, 2006), 5. Available at: www2.lse.ac.uk/internationalRelations/centresandunits/EFPU/EFPUpdfs/EFPUchallengewp3.pdf (accessed April 6, 2012).

83. James O Finckenauer, "Russian Transnational Organized Crime and Human Trafficking," *Global Human Smuggling: Comparative Perspectives*, David Kyle and Ray Koslowski, eds. (Baltimore, MD: Johns Hopkins University Press, 2001), 175.

84. Ibid., 172-175.

85. Ibid., 167.

86. James H. Anderson and Stephen R. Bowers, "Terrorism and Crime: Critical Linkages," Liberty University Faculty Publications and Presentations: *Paper 19, 2000*. Available at: http://digitalcommons.liberty.edu/gov_fac_pubs/19/ (accessed April 6, 2012).

87. LaVerle Berry et al., "Nations Hospitable to Organized Crime and Terrorism," Report Prepared by the Federal Research Division, U.S. Library of Congress (Washington, DC: 2003), 61. Available at: www.loc.gov/rr/frd/pdf-files/Nats_Hospitable.pdf (accessed April 6, 2012).

88. Georgi Glonti, "Trafficking in Human Beings in Georgia and the CIS," *Demokratizatsiya*, Vol. 9, No. 3 (Summer 2001): 382.

89. Russell D. Howard and Colleen M. Traughber, "The "New Silk Road" of Terrorism and Organized Crime: The Key to Countering the Terror-Crime Nexus," 378.

90. Ibid., 379-380.

91. Derek Lutterbeck, "The New Security Agenda: Transnational Organized Crime and International Security," PowerPoint Presentation, undated. Available at: www.docstoc.com/docs/46379133/Transnational-Organised-Crime-an (accessed April 15, 2011).

92. United Nations Office for Disarmament Affairs, "Small Arms and Light Weapons," undated. Available at: www.un.org/disarmament/convarms/SALW (accessed April 1, 2012).

93. Small Arms Survey 2010: Gangs, Groups, and Guns, A Project of the Graduate Institute of International and Development Studies (Cambridge, UK: Cambridge University Press, 2010), 22. Available at: www.smallarmssurvey.org/publications/by-type/yearbook/small-arms-survey-2010.html (accessed April 7, 2012).

94. U.S. General Accountability Office, "Combating Terrorism: U.S. Government Should Improve Its Reporting on Terrorist Safe Havens," *GAO-11-561* (June 2011). Available at: www.ncjrs.gov/App/Publications/abstract.aspx?ID=258469 (accessed January 5, 2011).

95. Yvon Dandurand and Vivienne Chin, Links between Terrorism and Other Forms of Crime (Canada: International Centre for Criminal Law Reform and Criminal Justice Policy, 2004), 13.

96. Ibid., 13, 20.

97. Glenn E. Curtis and Tara Karacan, The Nexus Among Terrorists, Narcotics Traffickers, Weapons Proliferators, and Organized Crime Networks in Western Europe (Washington, DC: Library of Congress, 2004), 22.

98. Ibid.

99. Seth Mydans and Ray Bonner, "Major Russian arms dealer arrested in Thailand," The New York Times, March 6, 2008. Available at: www.nytimes.com/2008/03/06/world/europe/06iht-07dealer.10775231.html (accessed April 17, 2011).

100. Ibid.

101. Louise I. Shelley, et al., Methods and Motives: Exploring Links between Transnational Organized Crime and International Terrorism (Rockville, MD: National Criminal Justice Reference Service, 2005), 35-39.

102. Kimberly Mc Cloud and Matthew Osborne, "WMD Terrorism and Usama bin Laden," Center for Nonproliferation Studies Report, March 7, 2001. Available at: http://cns.miis.edu/reports/binladen.htm (accessed April 17, 2011).

103. Ibid.

104. Elizabeth Neuffer, "Bin Laden sought nuclear matter," The Boston Globe, September 16, 2001. Available at: www.boston.com/news/packages/underattack/globe_stories/0916/Bin_Laden_sought_nuclear_matter+.shtml (accessed April 25, 2011).

105. "Report Links Bin-Ladin, Nuclear Weapons," Al-Watan Al-Arabi, November 13, 1998. See also Jack Boureston, "Assessing al-Qaeda's WMD Capabilities," Center for Contemporary Conflict Strategic Insights, Vol. 1, Issue 7 (September 2, 2002). Available at: www.einiras.org/pub/details.cfm?lng=en&id=34612 (accessed April 7, 2012).

106. Shelley, et al., Methods and Motives: Exploring Links between Transnational Organized Crime and International Terrorism, 35-39.

107. Desmond Butler, "AP Exclusive: Officials say crime ring has uranium," The Associated Press via The Guardian (UK), September 27, 2011. Available at: www.guardian.co.uk/world/feedarticle/9866962 (accessed April 7, 2012).

108. Ibid.

109. "Singapore Man Convicted of Conspiracy to Provide Material Support to a Foreign Terrorist Organization," United States Department of Justice Press Release, October 18, 2010. Available at: www.justice.gov/usao/md/Public-Affairs/press_releases/press08/SingaporeManConvictedofConspiracytoProvideMaterialSupporttoaForeignTerroristOrganization.html (accessed December 1, 2011).

110. "Singapore man sentenced to 4 years in prison for conspiracy to provide material support to a foreign terrorist organization," U.S. Department of Homeland Security, Immigration and Customs Enforcement Press Release, December 16, 2010.

Available at: www.ice.gov/news/releases/1012/101216baltimore.htm (accessed December 2, 2011).

111. "Rohingya Terrorist Suspects Captured," Bangkok Post, June 17, 2009.

112. "Legalizing Drugs: Will it Improve or Collapse the Economy?" Foreclosure Fish. com, February 16, 2009. Available at: www.foreclosurefish.com/blog/index. php?id=708 (accessed April 7, 2012).

113. "Terrorist Groups Increasingly Linked to Drugs, Officials Say," Washington File, March 13, 2002. Available at: www.au.af.mil/au/awc/awcgate/state/epf304.htm (accessed May 8, 2011).

114. "Trinidad and Tobago affected by flourishing Venezuela drug trade," Newsday. com, March 11, 2007. Available at: www.newsday.co.tt/news/print,0,53636.html (accessed April 7, 2012).

115. "Narco-Terrorism: International Drug Trafficking and Terrorism—A Dangerous Mix," Hearing before the Committee of the Judiciary, United States Senate, May 20, 2003. Available at: www.au.af.mil/au/awc/awcgate/congress/narco_ terror_20may03.pdf (accessed December 22, 2010. See also Shelley, "Organized Crime, Terrorism, and Cybercrime," 203.

116. Braun, "Drug Trafficking and Middle Eastern Terrorist Groups: A Growing Nexus?"

117. Ibid.

118. Schmid, "Links between Terrorism and Drug Trafficking: A case of 'Narco-Terrorism'?" The original quote is by Frank G. Shanty, 334.

119. Stakelbeck, "Drug Money Funding Chavez, Islamic Terrorist Groups."

120. Rollins and Sun Wyler, "International Terrorism and Transnational Crime: Security Threats, U.S. Policy and Considerations for Congress," 11.

121. Michael Braun.

122. Ibid.

123. Ibid.

124. Stephanie Hanson, "FARC, ELN: Colombia's Left-Wing Guerillas," Council on Foreign Relations Backgrounder, August 19, 2009. Available at: www.cfr.org/ publication/9272/farc_eln.html (accessed April 7, 2012).

125. "'FARC y bandas se prestan coca para cumplir con narcos de Mexico': Director Antinarcóticos," (interview with General Cesar Pinson), El Tiempo, September 12, 2010. Available at www.eltiempo.com/archivo/documento/CMS-7902854 (accessed April 7, 2012).

126. Ray Walser, "State Sponsors of Terrorism: Time to Add Venezuela to the List," The Heritage Foundation Backgrounder No. 2362, January 20, 2010. Available at www.heritage.org/research/reports/2010/01/state-sponsors-of-terrorism-time-to-add-venezuela-to-the-list (accessed April 7, 2012).

127. "'FARC y bandas se prestan coca para cumplir con narcos de Mexico': Director Antinarcóticos."

128. Kristian Herbolzheimer, "After Alfonso Cano's death, Colombia must rethink its path to peace," The Guardian (UK), November 8, 2011, Available at: www.guardian.co.uk/commentisfree/2011/nov/08/alfonso-cano-colombia-farc (accessed November 19, 2011).

129. Peter Canby, "Latin America's Longest War," The Nation, August 16, 2004. Available at www.thenation.com/article/latin-americas-longestwar (accessed April 7, 2012).

130. Herbolzheimer, "After Alfonso Cano's death, Colombia must rethink its path to peace."

131. Geoffrey Clarfield, "What Does Hezbollah do for a Living?" New English Review, December 2010. Available at: www.newenglishreview.org/custpage.cfm/frm/77084/sec_id/77084 (accessed May 12, 2011).

132. "Terrorist Groups Increasingly Linked to Drugs, Officials Say."

133. Chris Zambelis, "Mystery Surrounds Alleged Hezbollah Links to Drug Arrests in Curacao," Terrorism Monitor, Vol. 7, Issue 18 (June 25, 2009). Available at: www.jamestown.org/programs/gta/single/?tx_ttnews%5Btt_news%5D=35183&tx_ttnews%5BbackPid%5D=26&cHash=189f5df0cf (accessed April 22, 2011).

134. "Iran heavily cuts funding to Hezbollah, report says," M & C News, December 16, 2010. Available at: www.monstersandcritics.com/news/middleeast/news/article_1606160.php/Iran-heavily-cuts-funding-to-Hezbollah-report-says (accessed April 22, 2011).

135. Marco Vernaschi, "The Cocaine Coast," Virginia Quarterly Review, Vol. 86, No. 1 (Winter 2010). Available at: www.vqronline.org/articles/2010/winter/vernaschi-cocaine-coast (accessed April 22, 2011).

136. J. Peter Pham, "Emerging West African Terror-Drug Nexus Poses Major Security Threat," World Defense Review, January 28, 2010. Available at: http://worlddefensereview.com/pham012810.shtml (accessed April 7, 2012).

137. Stakelbeck, "Drug Money Funding Chavez, Islamic Terrorist Groups."

138. Ibid.

139. Assaf Uni, "Hezbollah funded by drug trade in Europe," Haaretz.com, January 9, 2010. Available at: www.haaretz.com/news/report-hezbollah-funded-by-drug-trade-in-europe-1.261091 (accessed January 17, 2010).

140. "Seventeen arrested on Curacao for involvement in Hezbollah-linked drug ring," Associated Press, via Guardian.co.uk, April 29, 2009. Available at: www.guardian.co.uk/world/2009/apr/29/curacao-caribbean-drug-ring-hezbollah (accessed April 7, 2012).

141. Ibid.

142. Zambelis, "Mystery Surrounds Alleged Hezbollah Links to Drug Arrests in Curacao."

143. Ibid.

144. Ibid.

145. Ibid.

146. The Hezbollah case study presented in this paper is paraphrased from an earlier case study written by the author and appearing in: "Illegal Drugs: A Global Crisis Degrading Security, Economics, Human Potential and the Environment," *Directed Study*, U.S. Special Operations Command, May 2011.

147. Scott Shane, "U.S. Denies Iran Claims That Saudi Plot Defendant Belongs to Exile Group," *The New York Times*, October 19, 2011. Available at: www.nytimes.com/2011/10/20/world/middleeast/obama-administration-denies-iran-claims-that-saudi-plot-defendant-gholam-shakuri-belongs-to-exile-group.html (accessed October 19, 2011).

148. Ibid.

149. Mark Rockwell, "Two Men Charged with Selling Heroin to Fund Hezbollah Weapons," *Government Security News*, November 21, 2011. Available at: www.gsnmagazine.com/node/25046?c=law_enforcement_first_responders (accessed November 22, 2011).

150. "Manhattan U.S. Attorney Announces Extraditions of Two Defendants Charged with Conspiring to Provide support to Hizballah," United States Attorney's Office, Southern District of New York, Press Release, November 17, 2011. Available at: www.justice.gov/usao/nys/pressreleases/November11/henarehsiavoshandaksucetinextraditionspr.pdf (accessed November 24, 2011).

151. Ibid.

152. Ibid.

153. Glenn E. Curtis and Tara Karacan, "The Nexus Among Terrorists, Narcotics Traffickers, Weapons Proliferators, and Organized Crime Networks in Western Europe," *Library of Congress Federal Research Division Report*, December 2002. Available at: www.loc.gov/rr/frd/pdf-files/WestEurope_NEXUS.pdf (accessed on November 19, 2011).

154. Hasim Soylemez, "PKK finances terrorism through drug trafficking," *Sunday's Zaman*, November 13, 2011. Availabe at: www.todayszaman.com/newsDetail_getNewsById.action?newsId=262462 (accessed March 1, 2012).

155. Curtis and Karacan, "The Nexus Among Terrorists, Narcotics Traffickers, Weapons Proliferators, and Organized Crime Networks in Western Europe."

156. Soylemez, "PKK Finances Terrorism through Drug Trafficking."

157. Ibid.

158. Ibid.

159. "Analysts: North African Qaeda helps drug trade," *Middle East Online*, June 15, 2010. Available at: www.middle-east-online.com/english/?id=39555 (accessed January 5, 2011).

160. Ibid.

161. Dario Cristiani, "Al-Qaeda in the Islamic Maghreb and the Africa-to-Europe Narco-Trafficking Connection," Terrorism Monitor, Vol. 8, Issue 43 (November 24,

2010). Available at: www.jamestown.org/single/?no_cache=1&tx_ttnews%5Btt_news%5D=37207&tx_ttnews%5BbackPid%5D=13&cHash=b9fb8c5a5e (accessed January 7, 2010).

162. Cristiani, "Al-Qaeda in the Islamic Maghreb and the Africa-to-Europe Narco-Trafficking Connection."

163. Ibid.

164. Ibid.

165. Logan, "DEA Uncovers Drug-Terror Nexus."

166. Ibid.

167. Ibid.

168. Donald E. Dekieffer, "Trade Diversion as a fund raising and money laundering technique of terrorist organizations," Thomas J. Biersteker and Sue E. Eckert, eds., *Countering the Financing of Terrorism* (London: Routledge, 2008), 156.

169. "Narcotics Enforcement," U.S. Department of Homeland Security Immigration and Customs Enforcement, undated. Available at: www.ice.gov/narcotics (accessed February 5, 2012).

170. William J. Krouse, "The Bureau of Alcohol, Tobacco, Firearms and Explosives (ATF): Budget and Operations for FY2011," *Congressional Research Service Report for Congress R41206*, January 6, 2011, 22. Available at: http://assets.open-crs.com/rpts/R41206_20110106.pdf (accessed April 7, 2012).

171. Ibid., 23.

172. Ibid.

173. "Illicit Tobacco: Various Schemes Are Used to Evade Taxes and Fees," *United States Government Accountability Office Report to Congressional Committees GAO-11-318*, March 2011. Available at: www.gao.gov/new.items/d11313.pdf (accessed Oct. 14, 2011).

174. Louise I. Shelley and Sharon A. Melzer, "The Nexus of Organized Crime and Terrorism: Two Case Studies in Cigarette Smuggling," *International Journal of Comparative and Applied Criminal Justice*, Vol. 32, No. 1 (Spring 2008): 43-64. Available at: www.publicintegrity.org/investigations/tobacco/assets/pdf/Nexus_of_Organized_Crime.pdf (accessed October 21, 2011).

175. Maarten van Dijck, "The Link between the Financing of Terrorism and Cigarette Smuggling: What Evidence is There?" *HUMSEC Journal* Issue 1 (2007), 6. Available at: www.humsec.eu/cms/fileadmin/user_upload/humsec/Journal/van_Dijck_Cigarette_Smuggling.pdf (accessed February 5, 2012).

176. Ibid., 10.

177. Kate Willson, "Terrorism and Tobacco: Extremists, insurgents turn to cigarette smuggling," *Center for Public Integrity iWatch News*, June 29, 2009. Available at: www.iwatchnews.org/2009/06/29/6338/terrorism-and-tobacco (accessed November 23, 2011).

178. Martin A. Weiss, "Terrorist Financing: U.S. Agency Efforts and Inter-Agency Coordination," *Congressional Research Service Report for Congress RL-33020*, August 3, 2005. Available at: www.fas.org/sgp/crs/terror/RL33020.pdf (accessed April 7, 2012).

179. Krouse, "The Bureau of Alcohol, Tobacco, Firearms and Explosives (ATF): Budget and Operations for FY2011," 21-22.

180. Ibid., 22.

181. "Contraband, Organized Crime and the Threat to the Transportation and Supply Chain Function," *Fia International Research Ltd.*, September 2001, 29. Available at: www.icde.org.br/artigos/contraband+and+transports.pdf (accessed February 5, 2012).

182. Ibid., 40.

183. Omer Elagab and Jeehaan Elagab, *International Law Documents Relating to Terrorism* (London: Routledge-Cavendish, 2007), 164.

184. Ibid.

185. Rollins and Sun Wyler, "International Terrorism and Transnational Crime: Security Threats, U.S. Policy and Considerations for Congress," 25.

186. D. Scott Broyles and Martha Rubio. "A Smokescreen for Terrorism," *United States Department of Justice United States Attorneys' Bulletin*, Vol. 52, No.4 (January 2004), 31,33. Available at: www.justice.gov/usao/eousa/foia_reading_room/usab5201.pdf (accessed April 7, 2012).

187. Ibid., 33.

188. Ibid.

189. Ibid.

190. Ibid., 34.

191. Donald E. Dekieffer, "Trade Diversion as a fund raising and money laundering technique of terrorist organizations," Thomas J. Biersteker and Sue E. Eckert, eds., *Countering the Financing of Terrorism* (London: Routledge, 2008), 157.

192. See Broyles and Rubio, "A Smokescreen for Terrorism," 21. Congress had just enacted a law making it illegal to provide "material support or resources" to a designated terrorist group.

193. Louise E. Shelly and Sharon Melzer, "The Nexus of Organized Crime and Terrorism: Two Case Studies in Cigarette Smuggling." *International Journal of Comparative and Applied Criminal Justice*, Spring 2008, Vol. 32. No. 1, 2.

194. Broyles and Rubio. "A Smokescreen for Terrorism."

195. Elagab and Elagab, International Law Documents Relating to Terrorism, 164.

196. United States v. Elias Mohamad Akhdar, Ali Mohamad Akhdar, Hassan Moussa Makki, United States District Court Eastern District of Michigan Southern Division. Available at: Findlaw.com.

197. Luk Joossens and M. Raw, "Progress in combating cigarette smuggling: controlling the supply chain," *Tobacco Control* Vol. 17, Issue 6 (December 2008),

399. Available at: http://tobaccocontrol.bmj.com/content/17/6/399.full (accessed October 14, 2011).

198. Shelley and Melzer, "The Nexus of Organized Crime and Terrorism: Two Case Studies in Cigarette Smuggling," 8-9.

199. Ibid., 9-10.

200. Soylemez, "PKK Finances Terrorism through Drug Trafficking."

201. Pacifica Goddard and Keith Nuthall, "Tri-border zone fuels illicit tobacco trade," *International News Services*, January 1, 2009. Available at: www.internation-alnewsservices.com/articles/36-archive/17234-tri-border-zone-fuels-illicit-tobacco-trade (accessed December 2, 2011).

202. Ibid.

203. Ibid.

204. Monte Reel, "Paraguayan Smuggling Crossroads Scrutinized," *The Washington Post*, August 3, 2006. Available at: www.washingtonpost.com/wp-dyn/content/article/2006/08/02/AR2006080201729.html (accessed February 5, 2012).

205. Goddard and Nuthall, "Tri-border zone fuels illicit tobacco trade."

206. Rollins and Sun Wyler, "International Terrorism and Transnational Crime: Security Threats, U.S. Policy and Considerations for Congress," 26.

207. Willson, "Terrorism and Tobacco: Extremists, insurgents turn to cigarette smuggling."

208. Ibid.

209. Stephen Harmon, "From GSPC to AQIM: The evolution of an Algerian Islamist terrorist group into an Al-Qa'ida Affiliate and its implications for the Sahara-Sahel region," *Concerned Africa Scholars Bulletin* No. 85(Spring 2010), 19. Available at: http://concernedafricascholars.org/docs/bulletin85harmon.pdf (accessed December 2, 2011).

210. Laurent Bossard, "Insecurity in the Sahel, the Arab Spring and trans-Saharan co-operation," Organization for Economic Cooperation and Development Sahel and West Africa Club, September 15, 2011. Available at: www.oecd.org/document/31/0,3746,en_38233741_38242551_48815839_1_1_1_1,00.html (accessed November 15, 2011).

211. The United Nations Educational, Scientific and Cultural Organization (UNESCO) has defined cultural property as "movable or immovable property of great importance to the cultural heritage of every people, such as monuments of architecture, art or history, whether religious or secular; archaeological sites; groups of buildings which, as a whole, are of historical or artistic interest; works of art; manuscripts, books and other objects of artistic, historical or archaeological interest; as well as scientific collections and important collections of books or archives or of reproductions of the property defined above." See "Convention for the Protection of Cultural Property in the Event of Armed Conflict with Regulations for the Execution of the Convention 1954," United Nations Educational, Scientific and Cultural Organization, May 14, 1954. Available at: http://portal.unesco.org/

en/ev.php-URL_ID=13637&URL_DO=DO_TOPIC&URL_SECTION=201.html (accessed January 4, 2012).

212. Raymond Fisman and Shang-Jin Wei, "The Smuggling of Art, and the Art of Smuggling: Uncovering the Illicit Trade in Cultural Property," *National Bureau of Economic Research Working Paper Series*, No. 13446 (September 2007). Available at: www.nber.org/papers/w13446 (accessed April 7, 2012).

213. Kimberly Alderman, "Honor Amongst Thieves: Organized Crime and the Illicit Antiquities Trade," 4, JD Supra, December 5, 2011, Available at:http://www.jdsupra.com/post/documentViewer.aspx?fid=eb5644ac-3046-4e9c-b84b-bed1fe660379 (accessed January 5, 2012).

214. Friedrich T. Schipper and Magnus T. Bernhardsson, "Archaeology in Conflict: Setting the Agenda," *Forum Archaeologiae*, Vol. 55, No. 4 (2010). Available at: http://homepage.univie.ac.at/elisabeth.trinkl/forum/forum0610/forum55schipper.pdf (accessed January 5, 2012).

215. "Cultural Property Crimes Program," U.S. Department of Justice, U.S. National Central Bureau of INTERPOL, undated. Available at:www.justice.gov/usncb/programs/cultural_property_program.php (accessed January 3, 2012).

216. Neil Brodie, "Focus on Iraq: Spoils of War," *Archaeology*, Vol. 56, No. 4 (July/August 2003). Available at: www.archaeology.org/0307/etc/war.html (accessed January 6, 2012).

217. Matthew Bogdanos, "Casualties of War: The Looting of the Iraq Museum," *American Association of Museums Museum News*, March/April 2006. Available at: www.aam-us.org/pubs/mn/MN_MA06_casualties.cfm (accessed January 4, 2012).

218. Arwa Damon, "Iraq museum pays smugglers for looted treasures," *CNN.com*, December 13, 2011. Available at: www.cnn.com/2011/12/13/world/meast/iraq-museum-paying-smugglers/index.html (accessed April 2, 2012).

219. Bogdanos, "Casualties of War."

220. Ibid.

221. Robert M. Poole, "Looting Iraq," *Smithsonian Magazine*, February 2008. Available at: www.smithsonianmag.com/specialsections/making-a-difference/monument-sidebar.html (accessed January 7, 2012).

222. Matthew Bogdanos, "Opinion: Illegal antiquities trade funds terrorism," *CNN.com* July 7, 2011. Available at: http://articles.cnn.com/2011-07-07/world/iraq.looting.bogdanos_1_antiquities-trade-iraq-s-national-museum-looting?_s=PM:WORLD (accessed February 5, 2012).

223. Alderman, 14.

224. Bogdanos, "Opinion: Illegal antiquities trade funds terrorism."

225. Roger Atwood, "The Loot Route," *Art News*, June 2008, 86-88. Available at: http://harrisschool.uchicago.edu/news/inthenews/cultpol-6-08.pdf (accessed January 6, 2012).

226. Ibid.

227. Charles Duecy, "Intelligence and Information Sharing in Counterterrorism," in D.G. Kamien, ed., *The McGraw-Hill Homeland Security Handbook* (New York: McGraw-Hill, 2006), 391-412.

228. "ICE Investigations: Mission Roles in Multi-Agency Areas of Responsibility," U.S. Department of Homeland Security Immigration and Customs Enforcement, August 2007, 2. Available at: www.fbiic.gov/public/2008/may/ICE_Mission_Roles.pdf (accessed April 3, 2011).

229. "Drug Interdiction," United States Coast Guard, August 1, 2010. Available at: www.uscg.mil/hq/cg5/cg531/drug_interdiction.asp (accessed March 25, 2011).

230. U.S. Customs and Border Protection Website. Available at::/www.cbp.gov/xp/cgov/about (accessed March 25, 2011).

231. See Chairman of the Joint Chiefs Instruction 3710.01 B January 26, 2007 Available at: http://www.dtic.mil/cjcs_directives/cdata/unlimit/3710_01.pdf (accessed March 12, 2012).

232. Thomas Harrigan, "The U.S. Security Homeland Security Role in the Mexican War Against Drug Cartels," Statement for the Record before the Subcommittee on Oversight, Investigations and Management, Committee on Homeland Security, United States House of Representatives, March 31, 2011, 1-5. Available at: www.justice.gov/dea/speeches/110331_testimony.pdf (accessed April 26, 2011).

233. Ibid., 2.

234. "Border safety concerns linger after Project Gunrunner revelations," *The Patriot Update*, April 6, 2011. Available at:http://patriotupdate.com/5187/border-safety-concerns-linger-after-project-gunrunner-revelations (accessed April 30, 2011).

235. Julian Aguilar, "Bill Seeks to Designate Drug Cartels as Terrorists," *The New York Times*, April 21, 2011. Available at: www.nytimes.com/2011/04/22/us/22ttcartels.html (accessed April 26, 2011).

236. Peter T. King and Michael T. McCaul, et al. "King, McCaul Letter to Secretary Clinton on Mexican Drug Cartels," U.S. House of Representatives Committee on Homeland Security, April 27, 2011. Available at: http://homeland.house.gov/letter/mccaul-king-letter-secretary-clinton-mexican-drug-cartels (accessed April 29, 2011).

237. King and McCaul, "King, McCaul Letter to Secretary Clinton on Mexican Drug Cartels."

238. Ben Buchanan, "U.S. Announces New Efforts to Combat Mexican Drug Trafficking Trade," *ABC News*, June 9, 2009. Available at: http://abcnews.go.com/Blotter/story?id=7786583 (accessed April 29, 2011).

239. Reel, "Paraguayan Smuggling Crossroads Scrutinized."

240. "Terrorism: How Have Other Countries Handled It? How Should We?" *Constitutional Rights Foundation*, undated. Available at: www.crf-usa.org/america-responds-to-terrorism/terrorism-how-have-other-countries-handled-it.html (accessed February 7, 2012).

241. Paul Wilkinson, *Terrorism Versus Democracy: The Liberal State Response*, 2nd Edition (New York: Routledge, 2006), 66-67.

242. Ibid., 67.

243. Matthew Levitt, "Hezbollah: Party of Fraud," *Foreign Affairs*, July 27, 2011. Available at: www.foreignaffairs.com/articles/67997/matthew-levitt/hezbollah-party-of-fraud?page=3 (accessed February 7, 2012).

244. Ibid.

245. "Country Reports on Terrorism 2007," United States Department of State Office of the Coordinator for Counterterrorism, April 2008. Available at: www.nauss.edu.sa/Reports/WTR_2007.pdf (accessed February 7, 2012).

246. "Tracking Narco-Terrorist Networks."

247. "Countering the Changing Threat of International Terrorism," *Report from the National Commission on Terrorism*, June 2000. Available at: www.fas.org/irp/threat/commission.html (accessed February 7, 2012).

248. Tom O'Connor, "Terror Financing." *MegaLinks in Criminal Justice*, January 3, 2012. Available at: www.drtomoconnor.com/3440/3440lect03asecure.htm (accessed April 7, 2012).

249. "Criminal Enforcement Against Terrorists," *Transactional Records Access Clearinghouse Report Supplement*, June 17, 2002. Available at: http://trac.syr.edu/tracreports/terrorism/supp.html (accessed April 7, 2012).

250. Ibid.

251. Ibid.

252. "Tracking Narco-Terrorist Networks."

253. Howard and Nencheck, "The New Terrorism," . As this article is going to press, the debate is swirling around the notion that "torture" had a positive effect on turning evidence on bin Laden's whereabouts.

254. Russell D. Howard, "Intelligence in Denied Areas: New Concepts for a Changing Security Environment," *JSOU Report* 07-10 (December 2007), 7. Available at: www.globalsecurity.org/military/library/report/2007/0712_jsou-report-07-10.pdf (accessed April 26, 2011).

255. Ibid.

256. Tim Newark, "Pact With the Devil?" *History Today*, Vol. 57, Issue 4 (2007). Available at: www.historytoday.com/tim-newark/pact-devil (accessed April 7, 2012).

257. Stephen Braun, Judy Pasternak, andSebastian Rotella, "Al-Qaeda Linked to Russian Arms Dealer," *The Los Angeles Times*, February 16, 2002. Available at: http://articles.latimes.com/2002/feb/16/news/mn-28372 (accessed April 7, 2012).

258. Richard Galpin, "'Kremlin Links' of Alleged Arms Dealer Viktor Bout," *BBC News*, January 20, 2011. Available at: www.bbc.co.uk/news/mobile/world-europe-12208961 (accessed April 26, 2011).

259. Douglas Farah, "Arrest Aids Pursuit of Weapons Network; Dealer Supplied Taliban, al-Qaeda, Officials Say," *The Washington Post*, February 26, 2002. Available at: www.highbeam.com/doc/1P2-324886.html (accessed April 7, 2012).

260. See Howard, "Intelligence in Denied Areas," 11. The author makes a similar argument concerning International arms dealer Monzer Kassar of Marbella of Spain (actually, he is Syrian), who was arrested on June 9, 2007 in Madrid for conspiring to sell millions of dollars' worth of weapons to the FARC.

261. Bartosz Hieronim Stanisławski, "Global Black Spots: Threats from Governance without Governments," *The National Strategy Forum Review*, Vol. 20, No. 3 (Summer 2011), 1-5, Available at: http://nationalstrategy.com/Portals/0/documents/Summer 2011 NSFR/Global Black Spots.pdf (accessed October 18, 2011).

262. Ibid.

263. Ibid.

264. Ibid., 2-3.

265. Rollins and Sun Wyler, "International Terrorism and Transnational Crime: Security Threats, U.S. Policy and Considerations for Congress."

266. Michael Evans, "War in Colombia,: Guerillas, Drugs and Human Rights in U.S. Colombia Policy," *National Security Archive Electronic Briefing Book*, No. 69 (May 3, 2002). Available at: www.gwu.edu/~nsarchiv/NSAEBB/NSAEBB69/part1.html (accessed April 23, 2013).

267. Ibid.

268. Mackenzie Eaglen, "Green Berets Value is Proven in War on Drugs," *The New York Times*, May 8, 2012. Available at: www.aei.org/article/foreign-and-defense-policy/defense/green-berets-value-is-proven-in-war-on-drugs (accessed April 23, 2013).

269. John Rollins and Liana Sun Wyler, "Terrorism and Transnational Crime: Foreign Policy Issues for Congress," *Congressional Research Service Report for Congress R41004* (October 19, 2012). Available at: www.fas.org/sgp/crs/terror/R41004.pdf (accessed April 30, 2013).

270. Ibid.

271. Federal Bureau of Investigation, "Frequently Asked Questions." Available at: www.fbi.gov/about-us/faqs (accessed April 30, 2013).

272. John Rollin and Liana Sun Wyler, "Terrorism and Transnational Crime: Foreign Policy Issues for Congress."

273. Ibid.

274. "ICE Investigations: Mission Roles in Multi-Agency Areas of Responsibility," U.S. Immigration and Customs Enforcement, U.S. Department of Homeland Security (August 2007). Available at: www.fbiic.gov/public/2008/may/ice_mission_roles.pdf (accessed April 30, 2013).

275. "National Security Investigations Division," U.S. Immigration and Customs Enforcement, U.S. Department of Homeland Security. Available at: www.ice.gov/national-security-investigations-division (accessed April 30, 2013).

276. U.S. Special Operations Command Publication 1 (2011), 21.

277. U.S. Code Title 10, Chapter 6, 167. Available at: www.law.cornell.edu/uscode/uscprint.html (accessed April 23, 2013).

278. John Rollins and Liana Sun Wyler, "Terrorism and Transnational Crime: Foreign Policy Issues for Congress."

279. For a very good review of SOF counter-trafficking operations, see Major Philip Brown, "USSOCOM's Role in Human Trafficking, paper from the U.S. Army Command and Staff College, School of Advanced Military Studies, December 2, 2010. Available at: http://cgsc.cdmhost.com/cdm/singleitem/collection/p4013coll3/id/2669/rec/5 (accessed April 23, 2013).

280. See U.S. Army Field Manual 31-20, 1990, 3-6. Available at: www.jezail.org/03_archive/manuals_monogrms/01_FM_31-20.pdf (accessed April 23, 2013).

281. "U.S. Army Special Forces Command (Airborne)," U.S. Army Special Operations Command. Available at: www.soc.mil/USASFC/USASFC.html (accessed April 30, 2013).

282. U.S. Special Operations, *Joint Publication 3-05* (April 2011), II-5. Available at: www.dtic.mil/doctrine/new_pubs/jp3_05.pdf (accessed April 30, 2013).

283. "U.S. Army Special Forces Command (Airborne)," U.S. Army Special Operations Command. Available at: www.soc.mil/USASFC/USASFC.html (accessed April 30, 2013).

284. Christina Wong, "Special Operations Forces to do More with Less," *Washington Times*, February 28, 2012. Available at: www.washingtontimes.com/news/2012/feb/28/special-operations-to-do-more-with-less (accessed April 23, 2013).

285. Lisa Wustholz, "FARC Weakened but Far From Dead," *Geopolitical Monitor*, November 24, 2011. Available at: www.geopoliticalmonitor.com/farc-is-weakened-but-far-from-dead-4543 (accessed April 23, 2013). See also: Dan Kubiske, "Forget Politics, FARC is Just Another Narco Gang," *Journalism, Journalists, and the World*, May 2, 2012. Available at: http://worldjournalism.wordpress.com/2012/05/02/forget-politics-farc-is-just-another-narco-gang (accessed April 23, 2013).

286. Carlotta Gall, "UN: Afghanistan Hooked on Drug Trade," *Chicago Tribune*, November 19, 2004. Available at: http://articles.chicagotribune.com/2004-11-19/news/0411190294_1_opium-drug-lords-poppy (accessed April 23, 2013).

287. Jamie Humphries, "Afghan Air Interdiction Unit Conducts First Integrated Counternarcotics Operation," North Atlantic Treaty Organization, August 10, 2011. Available at: a,www.aco.nato.int/afghan-air-interdiction-unit-conducts-first-integrated-counter-narcotics-operation.aspx (accessed April 23, 2013).

288. "U.S. Counter-Narcotics Strategy in Afghanistan," *Security Debrief*, October 22, 2009. Available at: http://securitydebrief.com/2009/10/22/us-counternarcotics-strategy-in-afghanistan (accessed April 30, 2013).

289. Ibid.

290. Thomas O'Connell, "Department of Defense Counternarcotics Budget," Statement before the U.S. Senate Committee on Armed Services, Subcommittee on

Emerging Threats and Capabilities, 108th Congress, April 2, 2004. Available at: www.dod.mil/dodgc/olc/docs/test04-04-02OConnell.doc (accessed April 30, 2013).

291. "The Pan Sahel Initiative," Global Security.org. Available at: www.globalsecurity.org/military/ops/pan-sahel.htm (accessed April 23, 2013).

292. "The Trans Sahara Counter-terrorism Partnership," AFRICOM Command Website. Available at: www.africom.mil/tsctp.asp (accessed April 23, 2013).

293. "Pan Sahel Initiative," Global Security.org.

294. "The Trans Sahara Counter-terrorism Partnership," AFRICOM Command Website.

295. U.S. Department of State and U.S. Agency for International Development, "Trans-Sahara Counter-terrorism Partnership," TSCTP U.S. Foreign Assistance Performance Publication (FY 2009). Available at: www.state.gov/documents/organization/159220.pdf (accessed April 23, 2013).

296. "U.S. Special Forces Help in Hunt for Kony," *Fox News*, April 30, 2012. Available at: www.foxnews.com/world/2012/04/29/us-special-forces-help-in-hunt-for-warlord-kony303902 (accessed April 23, 2013).

297. Xan Rice, "Background: The Lord's Resistance Army," *The Guardian (UK)*, October 20, 2007. Available at: www.guardian.co.uk/katine/2007/oct/20/about.uganda (accessed December 19, 2011).

298 "Lord's Resistance Army," *Global Security*. Available at: www.globalsecurity.org/military/world/para/lra.htm (accessed December 19, 2011).

299. "Lord's Resistance Army," National Consortium for the Study of Terrorism and the Responses to Terrorism (START). Available at: www.start.umd.edu/start/data_collections/tops/terrorist_organization_profile.asp?id=3513 (accessed December 19, 2011).

300. Ibid.

301. John Alexander, *Convergence of Special Operations and Civilian Law Enforcement*, Joint Special Operations University Report 10-6, July 2010, available at: citeseerx.ist.psu.edu/viewdoc/summary?doi=10.1.1.171.56 (accessed March 26, 2013).

302. Janice Burton, "Special Operations in Africa," *Special Warfare*, January-March 2013. Available at: www.soc.mil/swcs/SWmag/archive/SW2601/SW2601SpecialOperationsInAfrica.html (accessed April 23, 2013).

303. Ibid.

304. Ibid.

305. John Ryan. "Troops making progress in hunt for Kony." *USA Today*, May 29, 2012. Available at: http://usatoday30.usatoday.com/news/world/story/2012-05-29/joseph-kony-hunt/55260364/1 (accessed April 23, 2013).

306. James Kitfield, "Leading From The Shadows: The United States is using local soldiers to fight al-Qaida allies in East Africa," *National Journal*, March 9, 2013.

307. "Expanding the Nation's Option Set: The Future of Special Operations Forces," Center for Strategic and Budgetary Assessments, February 2013.

308. McKenzie O'Brien, "Fluctuations Between Crime and Terror: The Case of Abu Sayyaf's Kidnapping Activities," *Terrorism and Political Violence*, Vol. 24, No. 2 (2012), 320-336. See also Angel Rabasa et al., "Chapter Seven: The Convergence of Terrorism, Insurgency, and Crime," *Beyond al-Qaeda, Part 2: The Outer Rings of the Terrorist Universe*, (RAND Corporation, 2006), 101-160.

309. Beaudette, "JSOTF-P Uses Whole-Of-Nation Approach to Bring Stability to the Philippines, *Special Warfare*, July-September 2012. Available at: http://www.soc.mil/swcs/SWmag/archive/SW2503/SW2503BringStabilityToThePhilippines.html.

310. As quoted in Eric Schmitt and Thom Shanker, *Counterstrike: the Untold Story of America's Secret Campaign Against al-Qaeda* (New York: Times Books, 2011), 195-196.

311. Ibid.

312. Craig Whitlock, "Philippine President Aquino seeks U.S. military aid," *Washington Post*, June 8, 2012. Available at: http://articles.washingtonpost.com/2012-06-08/world/35462555_1_president-benigno-aquino-iii-clark-air-base-philippine-leaders (accessed April 23, 2013).

313. "Expanding the Nation's Option Set: The Future of Special Operations Forces."

314. Brian Bird and Gino Rullo, "U.S. Navy Special Forces help Honduras form elite counter trafficking force," United States Southern Command, February 3, 2013. Available at: www.southcom.mil/newsroom/Pages/US-Navy-Special-Forces-help-Honduras-form-elite-counter-trafficking-force.aspx (accessed April 30, 2013).

315. John Alexander, *Convergence of Special Operations and Civilian Law Enforcement*, Joint Special Operations University Report 10-6, July 2010, 65. Available at: citeseerx.ist.psu.edu/viewdoc/summary?doi=10.1.1.171.56 (accessed March 26, 2013).

316. Ibid.

317. "Expanding the Nation's Option Set: The Future of Special Operations Forces."

www.ingramcontent.com/pod-product-compliance
Lightning Source LLC
Chambersburg PA
CBHW080320290526
45790CB00005B/2119